I0105122

William Ralston Shedden Ralston, Ivan Andreevich Krylov

Krylof and his Fables

Fourth Edition

William Ralston Shedden Ralston, Ivan Andreevich Krylov

Krylof and his Fables
Fourth Edition

ISBN/EAN: 9783744777926

Printed in Europe, USA, Canada, Australia, Japan

Cover: Foto ©Thomas Meinert / pixelio.de

More available books at **www.hansebooks.com**

KRILOF AND HIS FABLES.

BY W. R. S. RALSTON, M.A.,

OF THE BRITISH MUSEUM

FOURTH EDITION.

CASSELL & COMPANY, LIMITED:

LONDON, PARIS & NEW YORK.

1883.

PREFACE TO THE FOURTH EDITION.

THE First Edition of this Translation of Krilof contained ninety-three Fables. To the Third Edition fifty-five more were added. As it now stands, the work contains all Krilof's original Fables, with the exception of a few, the principal charm of which depends upon the "curious felicity" of the fabulist's versification. It is sometimes better to leave verse alone than to turn it into prose. Krilof's direct imitations of Æsop and La Fontaine have not yet been attempted, their chief merit being one of form—a merit of which a prose translation can give no idea.

Athenæum Club,
August, 1883.

PREFACE TO THE FIRST EDITION.

—o—

THE poems of which a literal prose translation is now
offered to the English reader enjoy a popularity in
their native land which they can scarcely expect to obtain in
a foreign country. At home they live on the lips and in the
memories of old and young, of rich and poor, and have become a sort of national heirloom; abroad they run the risk
of being regarded as little more than quaint curiosities.
Much of their special excellence depends upon the choice
felicity of their language and the artistic structure of their
verse; it is, therefore, scarcely possible for any one to form
a fair idea of their original merits who makes their acquaintance only after they have been interpreted into alien prose.
But, even in a foreign dress, I think that they cannot fail to
interest and to please such readers as will make fair allow-
ance for the disadvantages under which they labour. Their
brilliance has naturally been dimmed, and their music has

been altogether stilled ; but their shrewd insight into the
thoughts and motives of the human heart, their ingenious
interpretation of the inarticulate sentiments which prevail in
the world of brutes, and their faculty of relating a story
clearly and concisely, all these remain ; and all these can be
appreciated by the foreign reader.   The pictures of Russian
life, also, which their words offer are perfectly intelligible to
all who take the trouble to study them, and will convey to
a stranger's mind a far more correct idea of Russian manners
and customs than he can gain from the cleverest illustrations
which fancy can suggest to an artist whose knowledge of the
subject is imperfect.   In the stories, for instance, of "The Two
Peasants," "The Peasant in Trouble," " The Three Moujiks,"
" The Peasant and the Labourer," and several others of
the same class, a store of information will be found respect-
ing the sayings and doings of the common people of Russia,
those many millions of fellow-Europeans of whom we know
much less than we do of the Chinese or the American Indians.
Still more interesting should be the protests which some of
them offer against the oppression and corruption which so
long prevailed in Russia ; against the manner in which the
strong trod down the weak, and the rich ground the faces of
the poor.   It is pleasant to mark the generous sympathy
with wronged weakness, the hardy indignation against guilty
strength, which prompted Krilof to pen such apologues as
those of " The Peasants and the River," " The Bear among
the Bees," and " The Dancing Fish."   Such stories as these
can never be entirely divested of their attraction, even when

they have been stripped of their ornaments and clothed in an unaccustomed and prosaic garb.

Most of the translators of these fables have tried to turn them into verse.* I have not ventured to attempt a similar task, but have confined my efforts to the production of what I hope is a faithful prose rendering of Krilof's poetry. The version may be disfigured by the ungainliness of a photographic portrait, but it aims at possessing something of a photograph's fidelity. The only liberty I have allowed myself with the fables I have selected for translation has been sometimes to omit the "moral" when it did not seem indispensable. Krilof is never tedious as a moralist, but all "morals" and "applications," and such-like tags and commentaries, are apt to become tiresome. I should not be surprised if the notes which I have myself added bore witness to the truth of this assertion.

I have translated about half of the entire collection of Krilof's fables. Of those I have omitted, a considerable part is composed of the imitations with which Krilof commenced his career as a fabulist, and of which I have thought it sufficient to give a couple of specimens. The rest are chiefly pieces which seem less original and characteristic than those I have selected, or which appear comparatively pointless now, though they had a special interest at the time they were written, and for the readers for whom they were intended.

---

* One of the exceptions is Mr. Sutherland Edwards, who has given prose renderings of most of the fables he has inserted in his excellent article on Krilof. It is to be found in his " Russians at Home "—by far the best English book about Russia [with the exception of Mr. Mackenzie Wallace's " Russia "].

It should be borne in mind that Krilof's fables were seldom mere literary bubbles, blown to create an instant's amusement or admiration, but not intended to serve any useful end, or to suggest any serious idea. Each of them, as a general rule, conveyed either a valuable warning or a wholesome reprimand.

Before bringing this preface to a close, I wish to acknowledge my obligations to the several writers from whom I have borrowed. For some reason which I cannot clearly explain, English translators from the Russian have shown a singular unwillingness to refer to the predecessors who have made their task comparatively easy. It has been a common practice to make copious, if not exclusive, use of a French or German translation of a Russian work, and then utterly to ignore the obligation. This course of behaviour appears to me injudicious, being apt to expose those who follow it to unpleasant comments. I think that, in translating from so unfamiliar a language as the Russian, one should by all means make use of such assistance as preceding translators have to offer; but let that assistance be frankly acknowledged.

In my own case, although my translations have been made from the original Russian, yet I have to express my thanks to M. Charles Parfait* for his spirited translation of the fables into French verse, and to M. Ferdinand Torney†

---

* "Fables de Krilof, traduites en vers français par Charles Parfait." Paris (H. Plon), 1867. 8vo.

† " Iwan Krylow's Fabeln. Aus dem Russischen von Ferdinand Torney." Mitau und Leipzig, 1842. 8vo.

and an anonymous German lady* for their versions into German verse—versions which are singularly faithful, considering the difficulties with which they have had to contend. For the sketch of Krilof's life I am almost entirely indebted to the memoirs written (in Russian) by M. Pletnef, by M. Lobanof, and by M. Grot, of the Academy of Sciences of St. Petersburg..

I gladly seize this opportunity of expressing my thanks to M. Grot for many kindnesses, and, among others, for his gift of the excellent and thoroughly exhaustive critique by M. Kenevich,† from which I have drawn most of the notes which I have inserted (between brackets) at the end of some of the fables.

Lastly, I have to thank another Russian friend, M. Alexander Onegine, for the trouble he has taken in revising my translation, thereby securing me against that dread of possible blunders innocently committed, which so often hangs like a dreary shadow about a translator's seldom over-enviable path.

W. R. S. R.

Inner Temple,
  Dec. 14, 1868.

---

* ' Fabeln von Krylow, treu übersetzt aus dem Russischen ins Deutsche, von einer Deutschen." St. Petersburg, 1863. 8vo.

† " Bibliograficheskiya i istoricheskiya primyechania k basnyam Kruilova. Sostavi V. Kenevich." Sanktpeterburg, 1868. 4to.

CONTENTS.

—o—

CONTENTS.

Page

THE TWO DOGS	157
THE STONE AND THE WORM	159
THE KITE	160
THE SQUIRREL IN SERVICE	161
THE PEASANT AND THE AXE	163
THE SQUIRREL AND THE THRUSH	164
THE ASS AND JUPITER	165
THE CAT AND THE NIGHTINGALE	167
THE PEASANT AND THE HORSE	169
THE GNAT AND THE SHEPHERD	170
THE WOLF AND THE CAT	171
THE CANNON AND THE SAILS	173
THE EAGLE AND THE BEE	175
THE LION	177
THE SWAN, THE PIKE, AND THE CRAB	178
THE CORN-FLOWER	179
PARNASSUS	181
THE LINNET AND THE HEDGEHOG	183
THE WOOD AND THE FIRE	185
THE TITMOUSE	187
THE MONKEYS	188
THE DUCAT	190
THE TRAVELLERS AND THE DOGS	192
THE PEASANT AND THE SNAKE	194
THE FLOWERS	196
THE FIRE AND THE DIAMOND	197
THE POND AND THE RIVER	199
THE EAGLE AND THE MOLE	201
THE STARLING	203
THE TREE	204
THE PEASANT AND THE FOX	206
THE GARDENER AND THE PHILOSOPHER	208
THE DOG	210
THE APE	211
THE CASK	213
THE NOBLEMAN AND THE PHILOSOPHER	216
THE HORSE AND ITS RIDER	217
THE GOOD FOX	219
THE COMMUNAL ASSEMBLY	222
THE TWO CASKS	223
THE FALSE ACCUSATION	224
THE FROG AND JUPITER	226
THE EAGLE AND THE FOWLS	227
APELLES AND THE ASS COLT	229
THE LION AND THE WOLF	230

MEMOIR.

———o———

RATHER more tnan a hundred years ago,* a boy was born at Moscow, on whom Fortune seemed at first by no means disposed to smile, but who was destined to enjoy in after-life a singular amount of honour and success. His father, a captain in the infantry of the line, found his income scarcely sufficient for the support of even a small family, and had no reason for hoping that the future would bring him better times.

Soon after the birth of the little Ivan Andreëvich, the captain's family followed his regiment into the east of Russia ; and, after a time, found themselves at Orenburg, in the midst of the troubles caused by the insurrection of Pugachef, the insurgent leader, who produced so great a disturbance by giving himself out to be the Emperor Peter III. That unfortunate monarch had in reality been assassinated several years before ; but a story had got abroad that he had managed to escape from death, and was living somewhere in concealment ; so

---

* On February $\frac{2}{14}$, 1768, according to general report : but some writers think he was born a few years earlier.

the minds of many men were prepared to accept Pugachef's daring statement. Accordingly, the impostor soon raised a numerous army, and for some time set the imperial troops at defiance.

During the period of his success, he attacked the fortress in which the elder Krilof was stationed, and was so enraged at the obstinacy with which it was defended, that he declared he would hang that officer and all the members of his family. They all ultimately contrived to escape; but tradition states that they were often in great danger, and that on one occasion, when they were halting in a village post-house, the little Ivan was hidden out of harm's way in a large piece of earthenware which stood in the cottage.

From Orenburg, they went to Tver; and there the captain, finding that his expenses were becoming greater than his income, retired from the army, and obtained a post in the civil service. A few years later, he died, leaving very little to his son, now a lad of fourteen, beyond a large box of books, which had followed him in all his wanderings.

After a time, the boy obtained employment in the public service, but of so unremunerative a nature that his mother determined to go with him to St. Petersburg, in hopes of obtaining a pension there as an officer's widow. All that she did obtain was a post for her son, with the salary of two roubles (about six shillings) a month.* He remained in

---

* Money went further then, of course, than it will now. For instance, the wages paid to the servant kept by Madame Krilof were two roubles a year only. Still the little household must have been often reduced to great straits.

the public service till the year 1788, when he lost his mother.

She has been described as "a simple-minded woman, who had received scarcely any education," but one of great worth and of considerable strength of character. She had done her best to obtain a good education for her boy, reading Russian with him herself, and making him, when he was studying French, read all his translations aloud to her—although she did not understand a word of the language from which they were rendered. By means of little presents and rewards, she induced him to study hard, and he soon took very kindly to books. The old volumes which had formed his father's travelling library he read over and over again with delight, and, from the perusal of the histories which were among them, his mind became full of ideas about classic Greece and ancient Russia. Vague ideas concerning the stage next began to float through his head, and, after a time, they shaped themselves into a drama, called the " Cofeinitsa,"* which he wrote (if the date of his birth may be trusted) before he was sixteen years old. This he offered to a bookseller, who gave him sixty paper roubles for it (about as many francs), or rather, at Krilof's express desire, books to that amount. The works he chose were those of Racine, Boileau, and Molière, preferring them to those of Voltaire and Crébillon. Years afterwards, when he had become famous, the bookseller gave him back the MS., which he

---

* A " Cofeinitsa " is a fortune-teller who looks for auguries in coffee-grounds.

had never published, and the poet re-read it with a pleasure not altogether free from regret.

The lad next turned his attention to tragedy, and produced a piece called " Cleopatra," which he showed to his friend, the celebrated actor, Dmitrievsky. The actor went carefully over it with him, and pointed out so many faults that Krilof gave it up in despair, and began another, under the title of " Philomela." This also, which was finished in 1786, and was printed nine years later in the collection of Russian dramas published by the Academy of Sciences, failed to meet with the actor's approval. So the young author gave up the drama for a time.

After the death of his mother, which took place when he was twenty years old, Krilof found himself entirely alone in the world, and free to occupy himself as he pleased. So he soon gave up his employment in the public service, and determined to devote himself to literature.

In partnership with a retired officer of literary tastes, who had a printing establishment of his own, he founded a journal, or rather a monthly satirical magazine, called the " Spirit-Post ;"* but, cleverly as it was written, it was not a commercial success, and, after a year, it stopped. By this time, Krilof had become the sole proprietor of the printing-press, which occupied a room in the house which then stood where the Oldenburg Palace stands now, close to the Summer Garden. Then he began to print a new journal, called the "Spectator,"†

---

* *Pochta Dukhof.*   † *Zritel.*

which lasted eleven months. Those were bad days for journalists in Russia, and the circulation of the "Spectator" did not exceed 170 copies.* As soon as it had run its brief course, Krilof started a third journal, under the title of the "St. Petersburg Mercury;" but, after a year's existence, this also came to a close, never having secured more than 150 subscribers. After its demise, Krilof discontinued his own publications, but he continued to print for others.

By this time, he had become well known in the world of letters, and, as he was also a good musician and an agreeable companion, he was much sought after in society. Most of his biographers relate that he led a jovial and careless life until 1801, when the Empress Maria Fedorovna obtained a post for him at Riga, under Prince Sergius Galitsin.† But M. Grot, of the Academy of Sciences, points out that this is a mistake. Krilof had, long before that time, become intimate with the Prince, in whose house he lived for a while at Moscow, and whom he accompanied first into Lithuania, and then to his country house in the province of Saratof, in South-east Russia. There he remained till the year 1801.

This was an important period in his life, for it enabled him to study the country well, and the ways of the country people.

---

* At that time, Karamzin's "Moscow Journal," the periodical which then had the largest circulation, could boast of only 300 subscribers.

† There are many princes of this name in Russia ; so many, that tradition relates how a nobleman who, one day, attempted to pass over a river in a ferry-boat without payment, claiming exemption on the ground that he was a Prince Galitsin, was indignantly addressed by the ferryman with the words, "Am not I a Prince Galitsin too?" And so he really was.

When at Tver, in his boyish days, he was always fond of associating with the common folk, the "black people," as they are called in Russia; and he would spend whole hours in wandering about the bazaars or the places where the moujiks were amusing themselves, or in sitting on the banks of the Volga, listening to the conversation of the washer-women who congregated there, and gossiped over their work. While at Prince Galitsin's he had again an opportunity of mixing among the peasantry, and of making himself thoroughly acquainted with the joys and sorrows of village life. There he could see for himself how hard was too often the peasant's lot, how heavy was the pressure under which he had to groan. It was there, in all probability, that he stored up those impressions of the country to which he afterwards so often gave form and colour in his fables. There, too, he was able to study the curious scene presented by a rich noble's country house; for Prince Galitsin lived in great state, keeping up a band of forty musicians to play to him, and employing altogether as many as six hundred retainers in his household. The Prince and all his family were very kind to the young poet, who used to teach the children of the house, and get up little musical and theatrical entertainments for the amusement of his hosts. The only things he had to complain of were the gnats and flies, which are certainly very trying in Russia, and particularly in the neighbourhood of the Volga, and which he used to try to avoid by mounting to the top of the village belfry, where he was one day found, fast asleep among the bells.

When the Emperor Alexander I. mounted the throne, in 1801, he recalled Prince Galitsin from his retirement in the country, and made him military governor of Livonia. Krilof went with him as a secretary, but did not long act in that capacity; for it soon turned out that he had no great talent for business, and, besides that, he began to devote himself to gambling with what seemed likely to be a fatal passion. But he stayed with the Prince, as a friend and companion, till 1804, when his patron gave up his appointment, and then he returned to St. Petersburg. According to the usual accounts, it was then that he went to the Prince's estates in the province of Saratof; but it seems more likely that he took to leading a wandering life at that time, and continued it for some years, going from one Russian city to another, as fancy led him. He is said to have won a very large sum of money at cards during his residence in Riga, so that he could well afford to be idle and extravagant for a time.

What is certain is, that towards the end of the year 1805 he spent some time in Moscow, and became intimate with the literary celebrities of that capital. To one of these, the celebrated poet and fabulist Dmitrief, Krilof one day showed some fables which he had adapted from La Fontaine. Struck by their spirit and animation, Dmitrief inserted them in the "Moscow Spectator," where they obtained a decided success, and strongly recommended their author to cultivate this style of writing. Krilof's fame may be said to date from that epoch. He was nearly forty years old before he found out in what his strength lay.

In 1806 he returned to St. Petersburg, and soon afterwards obtained a Government appointment, which he held for some years. In 1807 he produced two comedies, which obtained considerable success on the stage. The one was called "The Fashions-Shop,"* and the other "A Lesson for Daughters,"† and both of them were levelled against that taste for everything French, which was always so excessively distasteful to Krilof. With their appearance his dramatic career came to a close, and thenceforward he was content to base his reputation on his fables, of which the first collection, twenty-three in number, was published in the year 1809; and the second, containing twenty-one more, in 1811. In 1812 he was appointed to a very congenial post in the Imperial Public Library, which had just been reorganized and placed under the direction of his intimate friend, Olenine. The officers to whom the various departments were entrusted were all men of learning and literary tastes, and the section of Russian Literature was confided to Sopikof, a very learned authority on Slavonic bibliography. Krilof entered the Library as his assistant, and, six years later, succeeded him in his post and in his official quarters. That position he continued to hold till the year 1841, when he definitively retired from the public service. Long before that time his fables had made him the most popular writer in Russia.

The years he spent in the Public Library, almost thirty in number, glided peacefully away. He was a man of but few

* *Modnaya Lavka.*   † *Urok Dochkam.*

wants, and such as he had he could easily satisfy. Besides his salary, he had a pension of at first about sixty pounds a year, and afterwards of twice that amount; so he was sufficiently well off. His position in the literary and scientific world was a very pleasant one. His fame as a popular author was continually increasing, his presence was greatly prized and sought after in society, and he was treated with almost affectionate kindness by the imperial family. He might, if he had liked, have revolved in the most distinguished circles; but his tastes were very simple, and he had little sympathy with gilded magnificence. His quarters in the Public Library suited him admirably, and so did his post, in which he had little to disturb him. The rooms which he had inherited from his predecessor, Sopikof, were on the second floor of the building, their windows looking out on the Gostinnoi-Dvor, the principal bazaar of St. Petersburg—a huge collection of shops, the arcades surrounding which are enlivened all day by the presence of crowds of loungers or intending purchasers. From his rooms Krilof could look down at his ease on the busy scene below, and could listen contentedly to the conversations which were constantly going on there between the merchants and their customers, or among the peasants and the droshky-drivers, who are accustomed to loiter in picturesque groups about the street which divides the Library from the bazaar. After his official labours were over for the day, he used to go to the English Club, so called because it was originally founded by an Englishman, and there he would dine heartily, and then enjoy a doze. For some time after

his death, a certain stain, due to the pressure of his head
during the nap which was his "usual custom of an afternoon,"
was carefully preserved upon the walls of the club. When
his doze was over, he would sometimes go to the theatre; but
more frequently he stayed where he was, playing cards till it
was time to go home. As he grew older and more unwieldy,
he went out more rarely into society; but there were a few
houses which he always loved to frequent, especially that of
the Olenines, by whom he was treated as if he had been a
member of the family. In the literary, artistic, and scientific
circles of St. Petersburg it has always been possible to enjoy
the pleasures of society without encountering its drawbacks.
The idea of giving parties "out of revenge" has never been
able to naturalize itself there; and men of narrow means
have not thought it necessary to hamper their mutual inter-
course by restrictions borrowed from the code of opulent
festivity. Consequently, Krilof was able to spend a sociable
evening with his friends, whenever the idea occurred to him,
without being compelled to submit to such changes of dress
as would have sorely vexed him. For he was careless to a
fault in his costume. At home, he generally wore an old
and tattered dressing-gown, and he had a strong objection
to renewing his wardrobe. When his old clothes were worn
out, his friends used sometimes to get him invested in new
ones by dint of stratagem; but it was impossible to instil
into him the reverence with which such objects are generally
regarded by well-regulated minds. Gloves he never would
condescend to wear, even in the depth of winter. "I always

lose them," he used to plead, "and my hands never get cold." And, indeed, his circulation was singularly vigorous. When he lived near the Summer Garden, he used to bathe every day in the adjacent canal, and he continued this practice even when the water was covered by a thin coat of ice. So great was his contempt for clothes that, in hot weather, he would sometimes dispense with all but his shirt; and on one occasion, when, thus simply clad, he was playing the violin, he was so carried away by the tide of musical feeling, that he spent some time tranquilly performing at his open window—quite unaware that he was presenting a singular spectacle to the world of fashion then promenading in the Summer Garden. He had an eccentric habit of appropriating any stray napkin or towel, or the like, that might be lying about a room, and of afterwards producing it from his pocket, under the impression that it was his hand-kerchief, and waving it before the eyes of the astonished company. Perhaps the strangest story told on good authority of his absence of mind in things sartorial is that of his going to court on one occasion in a new uniform. His friend Olenine, just before entering the presence-chamber, thought it as well to scrutinize Krilof's costume, and discovered that he had got on so new a coat, that its buttons were still enveloped in the silver paper which the tailor had carefully wrapped round them.

The state of his apartments was in keeping with that of his dress. Neither order nor cleanliness had charms for his eyes. Nothing was ever cleaned or put to rights in his rooms : his books lay about anywhere ; undisturbed dust accumulated upon everything. He was very fond of birds ; and, twice a day, he used to strew his floor with oats, on which the pigeons, which haunted the adjacent bazaar— sacred birds to Russian eyes—would descend in flocks, finding easy access through the open window.

During one brief period, the rooms wore a totally different appearance ; but the change did not last long. Krilof had sold a new edition of his fables for a large sum of money, and did not know what to do with it. At first, he thought of spending it in travelling abroad ; but he soon gave up that idea. Then he determined to expend it upon the embellishment of his apartments. Upholsterers were called in ; sumptuous furniture was freely bought. The floors were covered with costly carpets ; silken hangings adorned the walls and windows. Choice pictures were hung up on all sides, flanked by mirrors in gleaming frames ; and, wherever an inch of standing-room could be found, there was placed a crystal vase, or a delicate statuette, or some fragile form of beauty in glass. The whole abode seemed transformed as by the wave of a fairy's wand, and the owner might well be excused if he felt proud of the change he had produced, when the newly decorated rooms were lighted up on the occasion of the feast to which he invited his bosom friends in honour of his apartments' metamorphosis.

But he soon grew tired of all this unwonted splendour. A few days after the inaugural banquet, one of his friends happened to call upon him, and found that he had returned to his old ways. The rich carpets were strewn with oats, on which a greedy flock of pigeons was feeding. Every time the door opened, away flew the birds in a hurry, upsetting the crystals, overthrowing the statuettes, shivering the glass into fragments. A very short time sufficed to reduce the room to its normal state of dirt and disorder, from which it never recovered as long as Krilof occupied it. Only, before the ruin took place, a sketch of this sumptuous study was taken for the Grand Duchess Maria Nikolaevna, which still preserves the memory of the fabulist's short-lived magnificence.

As may well be supposed, his servants were none of the best. An old woman, assisted by her daughter, waited upon him, and took care not to trouble him by any excess of housewifely zeal. Nothing was ever cleaned; not a book was ever known to be dusted. If a visitor arrived, he did not know where to deposit his hat in safety, nor where to find a seat from which he could rise unsoiled. Krilof never troubled himself about such superfluities as a writing-desk or a cabinet. Even such necessaries as pens and ink and paper were seldom to be discovered without painful research.

One of his friends, in describing a visit which he paid the poet, states that he found him smoking a cigar, which kept going out. Each time it went out, he called the servant-girl in to give him a light; so at last she brought a candle without a candlestick, dropped a little melted tallow on the table, and stuck the candle in it for her master's convenience. He was greatly addicted to tobacco, we may take this opportunity of observing, and would often smoke, says Lobanof, "from thirty-five to fifty cigars a day." It is to be hoped that they were cigarettes or papirosses.

It was dangerous, as might be imagined, to lend Krilof a book of any value. On one occasion, he was sitting at breakfast, reading a large and valuable volume he had borrowed from his friend and patron, Olenine, when suddenly he overbalanced himself, and, in trying to avoid a fall, he upset the coffee-pot over the book. Rushing wildly into the kitchen, he carried off a bucket of water, and began to pour its contents over the book as it lay on the ground. Seeing this, his scared servant-maid burst into the rooms of his colleague, Gnedich, and horrified him by the news that her master had gone out of his mind.

This, by the way, was not the only occasion on which his eccentric demeanour savoured of madness to vulgar understandings. Once, it is said, when he was very young, he was stopping in the country with Count Tatischef, when his host was suddenly called away to town. The Count, whose whole family was to go with him, allowed Krilof, at his own request, to remain where he was. As soon as the young poet found himself alone, he began to carry out an idea he had long cherished, and to lead a life as similar as was possible to that led by man in unsophisticated times. With that view, he gave up devoting any time to his toilette, discontinued shaving, and allowed his hair and nails to grow as they liked. Books, however, he did not discard; but, instead of reading them at home, he spent the entire day

over them in the garden. One day, as he was strolling
there, presenting a strange and hermit-like appearance, the
sound of wheels was suddenly heard, and, before he could
escape into the house, the Count and all his family, returning
unexpectedly, drove past the very spot where he was. Their
surprise may be well conceived. His confusion was probably as great then as it was on the occasion of another
misadventure which happened to him in early youth. When
he was first at St. Petersburg, he used to spend a good deal
of time at the house of his friend, the actor Dmitrievsky.
It happened that at one time his visits were discontinued for
a while, and during that interval Dmitrievsky changed his
quarters. One day, Dmitrievsky met his young friend, and
invited him to dinner. At the appointed hour Krilof, who
knew nothing about the change of address, appeared at the
wonted door. It was opened by a servant, who told him
that her master was out. " I 'll come in and wait for him,"
said Krilof, making his way into what had been his friend's
bed-room, and there unceremoniously going to sleep on the
bed. Now it happened that the rooms were then occupied
by a Chinovnik and his wife. Presently they returned
home, and the lady went straight to her room without
having learned that a visitor had arrived during her absence.
Her astonishment may be imagined when she discovered an
utterly unknown young man tranquilly slumbering on the
bed. The shriek which she naturally uttered on seeing the
sleeping stranger called her husband to her side, and awoke
the involuntary trespasser, who at first had some difficulty in

accounting for his totally unexpected appearance there.   It was certainly an awkward position to retire from gracefully.

To his next-door neighbour, Gnedich, he was greatly attached, heartily enjoying his society.   Gnedich had translated the "Iliad," and was fond of holding forth on the subjects of Homer's merits and those of Greek writers in general.   One day, Krilof, who was then fifty years old, talked about learning Greek.   Gnedich told him he was too old, that no one could learn a new language after such and such an age, and added various other similar remarks of equal value.   Krilof made no reply; but, the next day, he began to study Greek, making use of a New Testament in which the original was accompanied by a Slavonic translation, and being thus saved the trouble of consulting a dictionary. For two years he continued his studies in secret.   At the end of that time, he happened to be present one day when Gnedich was complaining that he could not understand a certain passage in Homer.   "I should read it this way," said Krilof, favouring him with an impromptu translation. At first, Gnedich thought he was being cheated; but when his companion had proved that he now knew Greek, translating several passages taken from Homer at random, he did not know how to express his wonder and admiration in sufficiently strong terms.   Afterwards, he induced Krilof to commence a translation of the "Odyssey," but it never went very far.   Krilof soon began to neglect his classical studies, and the large collection of Greek works he had bought was shoved under his bed.   Sometimes he would stretch out an

arm in search of an Æsop, but all the others were forgotten ;
and, at last, his housekeeper, seeing no use in such musty
volumes, used them up, one after another, to heat the stove.
A somewhat similar fate once befell a fable of his own. He
had read it aloud at a party, and forgotten to take away
the manuscript with him. The next day he sent for it,
but learned that the servants, having found a very shabby
roll of paper, had used it to wrap up candles in.

As he grew older and more corpulent, his natural laziness
increased, and it became difficult to induce him to exert himself. He used to lie in bed late, and, when he got up, he would
invest himself in a dressing-gown and a pair of slippers, and
often sit in his rooms till evening, dressed in little more than
that simple garb. When he was on duty in the Library, and
therefore confined within its walls for twenty-four hours, he
never grumbled at his lot, as Gnedich used to do, but would
lie on a sofa and read novels all day. He read all sorts of
trash, merely to kill time, and sometimes thought so little
about what he was reading that, when he had got to the end
of a story, he would begin it over again without recognising
it. The only occurrence which could rouse him to active
exertion was that of a fire. The moment he heard of one,
he would jump out of bed, and set off for the scene of the
disaster, willing to remain intently gazing at it as long as it
lasted. He seldom grew so excited in conversation about
any other subject as he was when he described the various
great fires which he had seen, especially that which took
place on the north side of the Neva, when the "camels"

for the ships were destroyed. Conflagrations are numerous and extensive in Russia, and in winter, when everything is white with snow, the effects produced by a large mass of flame at night are very fine, and the more lasting inasmuch as it is difficult to obtain water in any other shape than that of rock ice.

Towards the end of Krilof's stay in the Library, he was recommended by the doctors to take more exercise; so, in fine weather, he used to go for long walks, and when it rained he paced the galleries round the upper floor of the Gostinnoi Dvor. At first, the shopkeepers used, according to their wont, to pester him with invitations to purchase; and, one day, the occupants of a certain stall made a rush at him, and led him in triumph to their counter. Feigning acquiescence, he turned over all they showed him; but always demanded still more costly goods, until he had made them fairly turn all their stock upside down. Then, with many thanks for the interesting exhibition they had offered him, he made his escape. A little farther on, the same scene was repeated. Then the shopkeepers grew wiser: those who had been victimized indulged in that little laugh at their own expense, for which a Russian's sense of humour makes him almost always ready; and the rest still more fully appreciated the joke.

Some of Krilof's biographers have spoken as if his personal appearance had been well known to all his fellow-citizens; but this is evidently a mere figure of speech. One of them tells a story of how the fabulist was lunching off oysters one day—he was very fond of them, and it is said that he could dispose of eight dozen, "washed down with English porter"—when he discovered that he had left his purse behind. So he had to ask the proprietor of the establishment, whom he did not know, to give him credit. "Certainly, Ivan Andreëvich," answered the landlord. "What, you know me, then?" asked Krilof. "Of course," was the flattering reply; "every one in the city knows you, Ivan Andreëvich."

So far, so well; but another narrator adds that, as Krilof was on his way home, he stopped to buy some paper at a shop in the Gostinnoi-Dvor, just opposite his own rooms. When the parcel was handed to him, he said to the shop-keeper, "I am Krilof; I live up there. Please send up for the money." But the tradesman, with the unseemly materialism of his class, merely remarked, "How can one know all the people in the world? There's lots of them hereabouts;" and refused to part with the paper until it was paid for.

But, in spite of this tradesman-like ignorance, it is certain that Krilof was well known by sight as well as by reputation; and people used to point him out to each other, and especially to their children, as he walked along the streets. His fables were eagerly sought after by the editors of journals and magazines, and the collected editions of them which he published from time to time met with a large and steadily increasing sale. Between the years 1830 and 1840, the publisher Smirdine printed 40,000 copies of them in various forms, which found their way into all parts of the empire, and made Krilof by far the most popular author of the day. There was scarcely a child belonging to the educated classes who was not familiar with his stories; and they were written in so simple a style, and in such idiomatic language, that they were, for the most part, perfectly intelligible even to the totally uneducated peasant.   His sketches of village life, for instance, and his shrewd little illustrations of popular thought and feeling would be as thoroughly appreciated by the rude inhabitants of a hamlet in the interior, supposing that they had an opportunity of hearing them read or recited, as by the literary men whom Krilof used to meet at Jukovsky's pleasant Saturday-evening gatherings, or by his learned colleagues of the Academy of Sciences or the "Society of the Lovers of Russian Literature."

Nor was it merely in his own country that Krilof's name was known.   Various translators had given specimens of his writings to their respective countrymen; and, in the year 1824, a sumptuous edition of his fables was edited in Paris by Count Gregory Orlof.   A number of distinguished French and Italian poets co-operated in this work, rendering into their best verse the literal prose translations which were laid before them.   Many a version which pretends to be "from the Russian" has been really produced after a similar fashion, and the result has generally been as disappointing as that of Count Orlof's enterprise, "whose book," says M. Charles Parfait, "was one in which Russia could not recognise a single characteristic of her national poet."   Still it served to gain Krilof a reputation in France of which many of his con temporaries would have been very proud. He does not seem to have cared much about it himself; and on one occasion, when the proofs of a memoir of his life, which was about to be inserted in a French biographical dictionary, were sent to him for correction, he at first refused to trouble himself about them at all, saying, " Let them write what they like," and ulti- mately consented only to make a few slight alterations in them. For he was singularly free from that eager thirst after fame which so many really distinguished writers have felt. He always spoke most modestly about what he had done. "I am like a sailor," he said, on one occasion, "who has not met with any disasters, simply because he has never ventured far from shore." His early works he called the follies of his youth; and even of his fables, after they had gained the general applause of the public, he was wont to say very little. Many of them alluded to persons and to events about which many people must have been curious to know; but he scarcely ever told even his most intimate friends what were the particular objects of his satire; and, in most cases, the secret went with him into the grave. Of his manuscripts he was utterly careless. Before a fable was printed, he took the greatest pains with it, going, perhaps, as many as ten times over it, and never ceasing to revise it as long as there was a word in it he could improve or correct. But, after the printers had finished with his copy, he took no more interest in it. Of the collection of his manuscripts now in the Public Library at St. Petersburg, a great part consists of a number of rough drafts found by his friend Lobanof among the litter of a garret.

In February, 1838, Krilof's seventieth birthday was celebrated by his friends in a manner which could not fail to touch him deeply. A grand banquet was organized in the Nobles' Hall, at which three hundred of the most distinguished members of the cultivated society of St. Petersburg assisted. In front of his seat was placed his bust, crowned with flowers, and, at the end of the feast, flowers were showered down upon him by the ladies who occupied the galleries, and who were eager to do honour to their own and their children's friend. A laurel crown had been presented to him, and, as he was going away, a number of the students of the University crowded round him, asking for a leaf as a relic.

From that time forward, he may almost be said to have written no more. About a couple of years after the festival, he resigned his office, and moved from the Public Library to the other side of the river. There he lived for some time in the Vassily Ostrof, leading a very retired life, and gradually dropping more and more out of society. It was while he was there that a fire broke out, one night, next door. Every one else was naturally much alarmed; but Krilof took everything so quietly, that he would not even dress and go out until he had finished his tea and a cigar, nor would he give any orders about saving his books and memoranda.

After some time, he again changed his abode, and went to the extremity of the city, where he fitted up some rooms, from the windows of which a splendid view might be enjoyed.

There he proposed to lead a still more retired life than before. It would, perhaps, have been more lonely than he would have liked; for he had outlived most of the friends of his younger days, and he does not seem to have had a single relation with whom he was acquainted. At one period of his life, when he was young and poor, and, comparatively speaking, unknown, he had formed a strong attachment for a young girl, whom he hoped to be allowed to marry. But her parents objected to his poverty, and his hopes remained unfulfilled. Among his poems are to be found a number of lyrics addressed to Annette. They form the only trace that is left of the fruitless passion of his youth. In his old age, he adopted the children of his servant's daughter, Saveleva; but it is very likely that, in his declining years, he missed those little attentions by which a loved hand can do so much to make smooth the end of the journey of life.

His last illness was one of but short duration. He retained the full use of his faculties to the end; and his last words were, " Lord, forgive me my trespasses!" With them ended a life which was very dear to his countrymen. He died on November $\frac{9}{21}$, 1844, at the age of 76.

His funeral was celebrated at the public expense, and was attended by such crowds that the great church of St. Isaac could not hold those who wished to assist at the service of the dead. The whole of the Nevsky Prospect was thronged by masses of sympathizing lookers-on, thousands of whom followed the coffin, which, surrounded by the students of the University, passed slowly up the long street, and under the

windows of the rooms in which Krilof had spent so many
peaceful years, till it reached the cemetery attached to the
Convent of St. Alexander Nevsky. There the remains of
Krilof were deposited, by the side of the tomb of his friend
Gnedich, and within sight of that of Karamzine. Beside
him in the coffin his friends had placed the laurel crown
which had been conferred upon him at the time of his jubilee
banquet, and, in accordance with an urgent request which
he expressed before his death, a bouquet which had many
years previously been presented to him by the Empress
Alexandra Fedorovna. Soon afterwards a public subscrip-
tion was opened for the purpose of erecting a monument to
his memory, and the children of Russia, of all ages and
classes, united in contributing to it. With its proceeds an
excellent statue of the poet was set up in the Summer Garden,
within sight of the windows of the palace which now occupies
the place of the house in which his printing-press used to
work. There he sits in bronze, just as he used to sit in the
flesh, clad in his well-loved dressing-gown, an open book in
his hand. The pedestal of the monument is adorned with
bronze figures representing the various animals about which
he wrote ; and a couple of bas-reliefs illustrate two of his most
popular fables—" Demian's Fish Soup " and " Fortune and
the Beggar." Around the monument, which stands in a
circular open space, a number of children are always at play,
dressed in the picturesque garb which juvenile Russia affects,
and on them the poet seems to smile benignly as he looks
down from his easy chair above. It is a thoroughly national

monument—a somewhat rare object in Russia, where previous statues have for the most part greatly puzzled the natives, who call them *bolvani*—idols. That of Lomonossof, for instance, which stands at Archangel bareheaded and classically undressed, is a subject of great wonder to the peasants, who find it of a chilly and depressing appearance, as seen among the snows of an Arctic winter. But Krilof's statue is of an altogether different kind, having the merits of being characteristic and intelligible. It is a worthy memorial to a man who had, to a singular degree, gained the affection of his contemporaries, and who will probably retain that of their descendants. For many a score of years to come his memory is likely to be kept green in the minds of the children and the children's children of those little people who now play around his statue, in what is one of the most picturesque spots of St. Petersburg, when the sun is bright and the sky is blue overhead, and the trees of the Summer Garden are clothed in foliage that offers a pleasant shelter from the heat. At such a time it is very pleasant for any one who has read Krilof's fables, and who is not unduly depressed by the thought that the tide of aristocratic life has ebbed from the summer-smitten city, to sit in the grateful shade, and, as he lazily watches the gleam of palace walls through the openings in the hanging curtain of green leaves, to call up before his mental vision the varied scenes which the poet has depicted, and the quaint animal life with which he has peopled them. If it be a Russian who is thus indulging in day-dreams, the chances are that they will be crossed by some shadow of regret for old days gone by, and perhaps haunted by what seem to be echoes of a voice that is still.

KRILOF'S STATUE IN THE SUMMER GARDEN

KRILOF AND HIS FABLES

THE TWO PEASANTS.

"GOOD day, gossip Thaddeus!"
"Good day, gossip Egor!"

"Well, friend, how are you getting on?"

"Oh, gossip, I see you don't know about my misfortune. God has afflicted me: I have burnt myself out of house and home, and have been obliged to go about begging ever since."

"How ever did you manage that? That was a poor joke, my friend,"

"Just so. On Christmas Day we had a feast. I went out to give the horses their food, candle in hand. I must confess there was a buzzing in my head. Well, I don't know how it was, but I must have let a spark fall. I just managed to save myself; but my homestead was burnt, and all I had in it. Now for your story."

"Ah, Thaddeus, a sad piece of work! With me, also, it seems, God has been angry. You see, I have no feet left. I think it's a perfect miracle that I escaped with my life. I went to the cellar for beer. It was Christmas Day in my case too, and I, too, must confess that I had swallowed a little too much brandy along with my friends. Well, that I mightn't set the house on fire in my drunkenness, I blew the candle right out. But the devil gave me such a fall downstairs in the dark, that he made me a mere wreck of a man; and here I've been a cripple ever since."

"Blame yourselves, friends," said their kinsman Stefan. "To tell the truth, I don't think it a miracle that one of you has burnt his house down, and the other is on crutches. Things go ill with a drunken man, when he has a candle in his hand; but he is even worse off when he is in the dark."

THE EDUCATION OF THE LION.

TO the Lion, the king of the forests, Heaven gave a son.
You know how different from ours is the nature of
beasts. Among us, a child a year old, if it belong to a royal
family, is small and weak and stupid. But, by the time it
has lived a twelvemonth, a lion-cub has long ago left off its
baby-linen. So, at the end of a year, the Lion began seriously
to consider that he must not allow his son to remain ignorant,
not wishing that the royal dignity should be degraded in
him, or that, when the son's turn should come to govern
the kingdom, the nation should reproach the father on his
account. But whom should he entreat, or compel, or induce
by rewards to instruct the Czarevich how to become a Czar?

Should he hand him over to the Fox? The Fox is clever, but it is terribly addicted to telling lies; and a liar is perpetually getting into trouble. " No," thought the Lion ; " the science of falsehood is not one which princes ought to study." Should he trust him to the Mole? Every one who speaks of that animal says that it is an extreme admirer of regularity in everything, and that it never takes a step without examining the ground before it, and that it cleans and shells with its own paws every grain of corn that comes to its table. In fact, the Mole has the reputation of being very great in small affairs. Unfortunately, however, though the Mole's eyes are keen for whatever is just under its nose, it cannot see anything at a distance. The Mole's love of order is an excellent thing for animals of its own kind; but the Lion's kingdom is considerably more extensive than a mole-run. Should he choose the Panther? The Panther is brave and strong, and, besides that, it is a great master of military tactics. But the Panther knows nothing about politics, and is absolutely ignorant of everything else that concerns civil affairs. Pretty lessons indeed it would give in ruling! A king must be a judge and a minister, as well as a warrior; but the Panther is good for nothing but fighting, so it, too, is unfit to educate royal children. To be brief, not a single beast, not even the Elephant himself, who was as much respected in the forest as Plato used to be in Greece, seemed wise enough or sufficiently well informed to satisfy the Lion.

By good fortune, or the opposite—we shall find out which before long,—another king, the king of birds, the Eagle, an old acquaintance and friend of the Lion, heard of that monarch's difficulty, and, wishing to do his friend a great kindness, offered to educate the young Lion himself. The Lion felt as if a weight were taken off his shoulders; and no wonder. What could be better, as it seemed, than to find a king as a prince's tutor? So the Lion-cub was got ready, and sent off to the Eagle's court, there to learn how to govern.

Two or three years go by; in the meantime, ask whom you will, you hear nothing but unanimous praise of the young Lion, and all the birds scatter through the forests wonderful stories about his merits. At last the appointed time comes, and the Lion sends for his son. The prince arrives, and the king gathers all his people together, summoning great and small alike. He embraces his son before them all, kisses him, and addresses him in these words: " My beloved son, you are my only heir. I am now looking forward to the grave; but you are only just entering upon life, so I intend to make over my sceptre to you. Only tell me first, in the presence of this assembly, what you have been taught, how much you know, and in what manner you propose to make your people happy."

" Papa," answered the prince, " I know what no one else here knows. I can tell where each bird, from the Eagle to the Quail, can most readily find water, on what each of them lives, and how many eggs it lays; and I can count up all the wants of every bird, without missing one. Here is the certificate my tutor gave me. It was not for nothing that the birds used to say that I could pick the stars out of the sky.

And when you have made up your mind to transfer your power to me, I will immediately begin to teach the beasts how to make nests."

On this the king and all his beasts howled aloud. The members of the council hung their heads, and the old Lion perceived, too late, that the young Lion had not learned what was wanted—that he was acquainted with birds only, not knowing the nature of beasts, although he was destined by birth to rule over beasts, and that he was utterly ignorant of the knowledge which is most requisite in kings—the knowledge of what are the wants of their own people, and what are the interests of their own country.

[This fable refers to the education of the Emperor Alexander I. Catherine entrusted it to the Genevese La Harpe —a man of excellent intentions, but one who knew very little about Russia, and who set up his own little republic before the eyes of the future despot as the type of the most perfect commonwealth in the world. He filled the boy's head with ideas which would certainly appear to Krilof to be beyond a boy's comprehension; and when his pupil came to the throne, he wrote him a pressing letter from Geneva, urging him to give Russia a constitution, without waiting to make any preparations for its reception.

One of Florian's fables bears the title of "The Lion's Education;" and as it was translated by Dmitrief, it is very probable that Krilof may have read it. But there is very little resemblance between the two fables.]

THE BROOK.

A SHEPHERD by the side of a Brook complainingly sang, in his grief, of his sad and irreparable loss. His pet lamb had lately been drowned in the neighbouring river. Having heard the Shepherd, the Brook thus began to murmur indignantly:

"Insatiable river! how would it be if thy depths, like mine, were clearly visible to all eyes, and every one could see, in thy most secret recesses, all the victims which thou hast so greedily swallowed up? I think that thou wouldst dive into the earth for shame, and hide thyself in its dark abysses. Methinks that, if Fate gave me such copious waters,

I should become an ornament to Nature, and would never hurt even so much as a chicken. How cautiously should my waves roll past every bush, every cottage! My shores would only bless me, and I should bring fresh life to the adjacent valleys and meadows, without robbing them of so much as even a single leaflet. Then, in a word, I should perform my journey in a kindly spirit, nowhere causing misfortune or sorrow, and my waters should flow right down to the sea as pure as silver."

So spake the Brook, and so it really meant. But what happened? A week had not gone by before a heavy rain-cloud burst upon a neighbouring hill. In its affluence of waters the Brook suddenly rivalled the river. But, alas! what has become of the Brook's tranquillity? The Brook overflows its banks with turbid waters. It seethes; it roars; it flings about masses of soiled foam. It overthrows ancestral oaks: their crashing may be heard afar. And, at last, that very shepherd, on whose account it lately upbraided the river with such a flow of eloquence, perished in it with all his flock, and of his cottage not even a trace was left behind.

How many brooks are there which flow along so smoothly, so peacefully, and murmur so sweetly to the heart, only because they have but very little water in them!

—◇—

THE MILLER.

THE water began to dribble away through a Miller's dam. At first there would have been no great harm done, if he had taken the matter in hand. But why should he? Our Miller does not think of troubling himself. The leak becomes worse every day, and the water pours out as if from a tap.

"Hallo, Miller! don't stand gaping there! It's time you should set your wits to work."

But the Miller says,

"Harm's a long way off. I don't require an ocean of water, and my mill is rich enough in it for all my time."

He sleeps; but meantime the water goes on running in torrents. And see! harm is here now in full force. The millstone stands still; the mill will not work. Our Miller bestirs himself, groans, troubles himself, and thinks how he can keep the waters back. While he is here on the dam, examining the leak, he observes his fowls coming to drink at the river.

"You stupid, good-for-nothing birds!" he cries. "I don't know where I'm to get water, even when you are out of the question; and here you come and drink the little that remains."

So he begins pelting them with faggots. What good did he do himself by this? Without a fowl left, or a drop of water, he went back home.

I have sometimes remarked that there are many proprietors of this kind—and this little fable was composed as a present for them—who do not grudge thousands spent on follies, but who think that they maintain domestic economy by collecting their candle-ends, and are ready to quarrel with their servants about them. With such economy, is it strange that houses rapidly fall utterly to pieces?

[It is said that Krilof's own ideas of economy were, for the most part, of the very kind he satirizes here. "Returning from a party with me one evening," says his friend Gniedich, "Krilof wouldn't pay what I did for a good carriage, saying it was wasting money. So he walked half

of the way home; but then he became tired, and eventually
he was obliged to get into a wretched vehicle, and pay
almost as much, for half the distance, as he had been asked
at first. And this was what he called economy."]

ONCE, in the days of old, a certain Grandee passed from his richly dight bed into the realm which Pluto sways. To speak more simply, he died. And so, as was anciently the custom, he appeared before the justice-seat of Hades. Straightway he was asked, "Where were you born? What have you been?"

"I was born in Persia, and my rank was that of a Satrap. But, as my health was feeble during my lifetime, I never exercised any personal control in my province, but left everything to be done by my secretary."

"But you—what did you do?"

"I ate, drank, and slept; and I signed everything he set before me."

"In with him, then, at once into Paradise!"

"How now! Where is the justice of this?" thereupon exclaimed Mercury, forgetting all politeness.

"Ah, brother," answered Eacus, "you know nothing about it. But don't you see this? The dead man was a fool. What would have happened if he, who had such power in his hands, had unfortunately interfered in business? Why, he would have ruined the whole province. The tears which would have flowed then would have been beyond all calculation. Therefore it is that he has gone into Paradise, because he did not interfere with business."

I was in court yesterday, and I saw a judge there. There can be no doubt that he will go into Paradise.

[When this fable was submitted to the censors, they sent it on to the Minister of Public Instruction, who kept it by him for a whole year, instead of giving any decision about it. Meanwhile, copies of it were circulated in MS., and it became well known in society; but still the minister withheld permission to print it. At last, at one of the court-masquerades, Krilof found an opportunity of reading it to the Emperor Nicholas, who was so delighted with it that he took him in his arms, kissed him, and said, " Write away, old man, write away." On the strength of this, Krilof applied anew to the authorities, and obtained leave to print the fable. With its appearance, his literary career may be said to have come to a close.]

THE WOLF IN THE KENNEL.

A WOLF, one night, thinking to climb into a sheepfold, fell into a kennel. Immediately the whole kennel was up in arms. The dogs, scenting the grisly disturber so near at hand, began to bark in their quarters, and to tear out to the fight.

"Hallo, lads, a thief!" cried the keepers; and immediately the gates were shut. In a moment the kennel became a hell. Men come running, one armed with a club, another with a gun. "Lights!" they cry; "bring lights!" The lights being brought, our Wolf is seen sitting squeezed up in the furthest corner, gnashing its teeth, its hide bristling, and its eyes looking as if it would fain eat up the whole party. Seeing, however, that it is not now in the presence of the flock, and that it is now called upon to pay the penalty for the sheep it has killed, my trickster resorts to negotiation, beginning thus :

" Friends, what is all this fuss about ?   I am your ancient gossip and comrade ; and I have come here to contract an alliance with you—not with the slightest intention of quarrelling.   Let us forget the past, and declare in favour of mutual harmony.   Not only will I for the future avoid touching the flocks belonging to this spot, but I will gladly fight in their behalf against others ; and I swear on the word of a Wolf that I—— "

" Listen, neighbour," here interrupted the huntsman. " You are grey-coated ; but I, friend, am grey-headed, and I have long known what your wolfish natures are like, and therefore it is my custom never to make peace with wolves until I have torn their skin from off their backs."

With that he let go the pack of hounds on the Wolf.

[This fable, which was printed in October, 1812, represents Napoleon in Russia. The words put into the mouth of the Wolf are almost exactly those of which he himself made use. It is said that, after the battle of Krasnoe, Kutuzof read this fable aloud to the officers who stood round him, and that, when he came to the words, " You are grey-coated ; but I, friend, am grey-headed," in which an allusion is made to Napoleon's grey overcoat and his own white hair, he took off his white forage-cap, and shook his bent head.   Buistrof says that he once read to Krilof a statement to the effect that, "after Borodino, Kutuzof's young soldiers abused him for not instantly attacking Napoleon ; but Krilof, understanding his intentions, sent him this fable, which he read to his younger officers, and so appeased them." On hearing this, however, Krilof frowned, and said, "That's all nonsense. Is it likely that I, a private individual, neither a diplomatist nor a soldier, should have known beforehand what Kutuzof was going to do? It's absurd ! Say, in some paper or other, my friend, that it is not true."

THE THREE MOUJIKS.

THREE Moujiks * stopped at a village to pass the night. They had done their business at Petersburg as drivers; had sometimes worked, and sometimes amused themselves; and were now going back to their native place. As a Moujik does not like to go to bed empty, our visitors asked for supper. But villagers have no variety of dishes. They set on the table before the hungry travellers a basin of cabbage soup, some bread, and the remains of a bowl of porridge. It wasn't like Petersburg fare, but there was no use in talk-

* Peasants.

2

ing about that ; at all events, it was better than going to bed
hungry. So the Moujiks crossed themselves, and sat down to
table. Then the one who was the sharpest of them, seeing
that there was altogether but little for three, perceived how
the business might be mended. When force can't win the
day, a little cunning must be tried.

"Comrades," he cries, "you know Thomas ; well, he 's
likely to have his hair cropped * during this levy."

"What levy ? "

" Why, there 's news of a war with China. Our father † has
ordered the Chinese to pay a tribute of tea."

On that the two others took to weighing the matter, and
deliberating upon it (unfortunately they could read, and had
studied newspapers and reports), as to how the war would be
carried on, and who should have the command. Our friends
began a regular discussion, surmised, explained, wrangled.
That was just what our trickster wanted. While they were
giving their advice, and settling affairs, and arranging the
forces, he didn't say a word. but ate up the whole of the
soup and the porridge.

---

* To be taken as a soldier.   † The Emperor.

THE DIVISION.

CERTAIN honest merchants, who had their dwelling and their counting-house in common, made a heap of money. Having wound up their business, they wish to divide their gains. But how can a division take place without squabbling? They have begun to quarrel about the money and the stock, when suddenly there is a cry that the house is on fire.

"Quick, quick, save the goods and the house!" shouts one of them. "Come along; we will settle our accounts afterwards!"

2—2

"Give me another thousand first!" screams a second, "or I will not stir from the spot."

"You have given me two thousand too little!" exclaims a third; "but here are my accounts, all perfectly straight."

"No, no; we protest against such an idea. How, for what, and why, do you claim that?"

Forgetting that the house was on fire, these strange fellows went on squabbling where they were, till they were suffocated by the smoke, and they and their goods were all burnt up together.

[This fable is said to refer to the squabbles which took place among the Russian generals at the time of the French invasion. Count Rostopchin, for instance, withdrew from the Moscow Volunteer Committee simply because it was made dependent on the Volunteer Committee of St. Petersburg. In many cases what was much worse than squabbling took place, some of the officials being charged with having, even at that critical period, "stolen all that could be stolen, the very clothes, the very food of the recruits, of the volunteers, of the prisoners."]

THE CROW AND THE HEN.

WHEN the Prince of Smolensk,* using skill as a weapon against insolence, laid a snare for the modern Vandals, and left them Moscow for their ruin, then all its inhabitants, old and young, assembled together without loss of time, and departed from the city, like a swarm of bees leaving their hive. On all the disquiet which then took place a Crow looked down tranquilly from a housetop, whetting its beak the while.

"What! are not you ready to start, gossip?" cried a Hen to it from a passing cart. "Why, they say the enemy is at our very gates."

---

* Kutusof. He received the title of Smolensky after the battle of **Krasnoe**.

"What is that to me?" replied the bird of omen. "I shall remain here quietly. You and your sisters can do as you please. But people don't boil crows, or roast them either; so I shall have no difficulty in living on good terms with the new-comers. It may even happen, perhaps, that I may get some cheese from them, or a stray bone, or something or other. Farewell, my fowl! a happy journey to you."

The Crow really did stay; but, instead of its gaining anything by doing so, when the time came in which the Prince of Smolensk began to starve his guests, it was itself seized by them, and turned into soup.

[This fable was printed in the magazine called "The Son of the Fatherland," in November, 1812. Towards the end of September in that year, news began to reach St. Petersburg of the miserable state of Napoleon's army. "Eye-witnesses assert," said the preceding number of the magazine, "that the French go out to shoot crows every day, and cannot sufficiently praise their *soupe aux corbeaux.*" In the same number appeared a caricature, styled "French crow-soup," representing four grenadiers, wounded, ragged, and emaciated, one of whom is plucking a crow, while the others are getting ready a carving-knife and a saucepan. When Murat's travelling kitchen fell into the hands of the Russians, the saucepans were full of horse and cat flesh. Later on in the retreat, a time came when some of the starving soldiers actually preyed on the dead bodies of their comrades.]

THE PEBBLE AND THE DIAMOND.

A DIAMOND, which some one had lost, lay for some time on the high road. At last it happened that a merchant picked it up. By him it was offered to the king, who bought it, had it set in gold, and made it one of the ornaments of the royal crown. Having heard of this, a Pebble began to make a fuss. The brilliant fate of the Diamond fascinated it; and, one day, seeing a Moujik passing, it besought him thus:

"Do me a kindness, fellow-countryman, and take me with you to the capital. Why should I go on suffering here in rain and mud, while our Diamond is, men say, in honour there? I don't understand why it has been treated with such respect. Side by side with me here it lay so many years; it is just such a stone as I am—my close companion. Do take me! How can one tell? If I am seen there, I too, perhaps, may be found worthy of being turned to account."

The Moujik took the stone into his lumbering cart, and conveyed it to the city. Our stone tumbled into the cart, thinking that it would soon be sitting by the side of the Diamond. But a quite different fate befell it. It really was turned to account, but only to mend a hole in the road.

THE MISER.

A CERTAIN Goblin used to keep watch over a rich treasure buried underground. Suddenly, he was ordered by the ruler of the demons to fly away for many years to the other side of the world. His service was of such a nature, that he was obliged to do as he was bid, whether he liked it or not. Our Goblin fell into a terrible perplexity, wondering how he should preserve his treasure in his absence—who there was to take charge of it. To build a treasure-house, and hire a guardian—that would cost much money. To leave it to itself—that way it might be lost. Impossible to answer for it for a day. Some one might dig it up, and steal it: people are quick at scenting out money.

He worried himself; he pondered over it; and at last an idea came into his head. The master of the house to which he was attached was a terrible Miser. The Goblin, having dug up the treasure, appeared to the Miser, and said,

"Dear master, they have ordered me to go away from your house to a distant land. But I have always been well disposed towards you, so don't refuse to accept this treasure of mine, as a parting token of affection. Eat, drink, and be merry, and spend it without fear; only, when you die, I am to be your sole heir. That is my single stipulation. As for the rest, may destiny grant you health and long life."

He spoke, and was off.

Ten—twenty years went by. Having completed his service, the Goblin flies home to his native land. What does he see? O rapturous sight! The Miser, dead from starvation, lies stretched on the strong box, its key in his hand; and the ducats are all there intact. So the Goblin gets his treasure back again, and rejoices greatly to think that it has had a guardian who did not cost him a single farthing.

[Krilof's remark at the end of this fable is—

"When a miser has money, and yet grudges to pay for food and drink, is he not treasuring up his ducats for a goblin?"

M. Parfait, the author of an excellent French translation of the fables, observes that the same idea has been expressed by a popular French poet, Pierre Dupont, who is not very likely to have read Krilof:

"Tirez profit de cette fable,
Vous tous qui rognez sur un liard ;
Vous thésaurisez pour le diable."

The goblin of the fable is the *domovoi*, or domestic spirit, in whom the Russian peasant has great faith. It is, probably, a near relation of the lubber-fiend which, in Milton's country house,

"Basks at the fire its hairy strength,"

and of the well-known Scotch bogle, which, when its weary landlord was *flitting* in order to get rid of it, exclaimed, from the centre of the furniture-laden cart, "And I'm flittin', too."]

THE PIKE AND THE CAT.

A CONCEITED Pike took it into its head to exercise the functions of a cat. I do not know whether the Evil One had plagued it with envy, or whether, perhaps, it had grown tired of fishy fare ; but, at all events, it thought fit to ask the Cat to take it out to the chase, with the intention of catching a few mice in the warehouse. " But, my dear friend," Vaska says to the Pike, " do you understand that kind of work? Take care, gossip, that you don't incur disgrace. It isn't without reason that they say, ' The work ought to be in the master's power.' "

"Why really, gossip, what a tremendous affair it is !

Mice, indeed! Why, I have been in the habit of catching perches!"

"Oh, very well. Come along!"

They went; they lay each in ambush. The Cat thoroughly enjoyed itself; made a hearty meal; then went to look after its comrade. Alas! the Pike, almost destitute of life, lay there gasping, its tail nibbled away by the mice. So the Cat, seeing that its comrade had undertaken a task quite beyond its strength, dragged it back, half dead, to its pond.

[The Pike, in this fable, represents Admiral Tchichakof, who, although a naval officer, was entrusted with the command of the troops intended to prevent Napoleon from crossing the Berezina during the retreat from Moscow. With this view he was stationed at Borisof; but the French surprised him there, and drove him out of the place, thereby securing the passage of the river. Sir Robert Wilson says the admiral was at dinner when the enemy broke in upon his rear-guard, captured the whole of his correspondence, and inflicted great loss on his troops.

In the Public Library at St. Petersburg is a collection of caricatures relating to the French invasion of Russia, one of which represents Kutuzof holding one end of a long net; Napoleon, in the form of a hare, is slipping out at the other end, which is held by Tchichakof, who is exclaiming, "*Je le sauve.*"

Tchichakof is said to have been "an Englishman in character;" he had learnt navigation in England, and had married an English woman. "To a sailor's bluntness he added the English reserve;" and this made his countrymen dislike him from the first. After the affair of the Berezina, they despised him also.]

THE ASS AND THE NIGHTINGALE.

A N Ass happened to see a Nightingale, one day, and said
to it,

"Listen, my dear. They say you have a great mastery
over song. I have long wished very much to hear you sing,
and to judge as to whether your talent is really so great."

On this the Nightingale began to make manifest its art—
whistled in countless ways, sobbed, sustained notes, passed
from one song to another; at one time let her voice die away,
and echoed the distant murmur of the languishing reed ; at
another, poured through the wood a shower of tiny notes.
Then all listened to the favourite singer of Aurora. The
breezes died away; the feathered choir was hushed; the cattle
lay down on the grass. Scarcely breathing, the shepherd
revelled in it, and only now and then, as he listened to it,
smiled on the shepherdess.

At length the singer ended. Then the Ass, bending its
head towards the ground, observed,

"It's tolerable. To speak the truth, one can listen to you
without being bored. But it's a pity you don't know our
Cock. You would sing a great deal better if you were to
take a few lessons from him."

Having heard such a judgment, our poor Nightingale took
to its wings and flew far away.

[It is said that Krilof wrote this fable after an interview with some great man (Count Razumofsky or Prince A. N. Galitzin, perhaps), who had asked him to read him some of his fables. After hearing them, the noble patron of letters said, " That is very good ; but why don't you translate, as Dmitrief does ?" " I cannot," modestly answered the poet, who returned home, and straightway wrote down the grandee an ass.

M. Fleury ranks this piece among the imitations ; and it is true that the same subject has been admirably treated by Diderot. But the idea may easily have occurred to Krilof without his having read Diderot's excellent fable.]

THE HOP-PLANT.

A HOP-PLANT had made its way to the edge of a garden, and had begun to wind itself around a dry stake in the fence. Now, in the open field beyond stood an oak-sapling.

"What use is there in that stunted creature, or, indeed, in any of its kind?" Thus about the oak the Hop used to whisper to the stake. "How can it even be compared with you? You, simply by your erect carriage, look like a perfect lady in its presence. It is true that it is clothed with foliage; but how rough it is! what a colour it has! Why ever does the earth nourish it?"

Meanwhile, a week had scarcely passed, before the owner broke up that stake for firewood, and transplanted the young oak into his garden.. His care resulted in full success, and the oak flourished, extending vigorous shoots. Remarking this, our Hop-plant wound itself about it, and now its voice is entirely devoted to the oak's glory and honour.

TRISHKA'S caftan was out at elbows. Why should he ponder long over it? He took to his needle, cut a quarter off each sleeve; so mended the elbows. The caftan was all right again, only his arms were bare for a quarter of their length. That is no great matter; but every one is always laughing at Trishka. So Trishka says,

"As I'm no fool, I'll set this affair straight also. I'll make the sleeves longer than they were before. Oh! Trishka is no common-place fellow."

So he cut off the skirts of his caftan, and used them to lengthen his sleeve. Then Trishka was happy, though he had a caftan which was as short as a waistcoat. In a similar way have I sometimes seen other embarrassed people set their affairs straight. Take a look at them as they dash away. They have all got on Trishka's caftan.

.

[An allusion to the ruinous shifts to which the Russian proprietors used to have recourse when their affairs became at all embarrassed. They are beginning to be less improvident now ; but, at the time when Krilof wrote the fable, they used to be notorious for their readiness to adopt any means which would afford them a temporary relief. It may easily be imagined how the unfortunate peasants must have suffered whenever their masters were seized by one of these reckless fits.]

THE ELEPHANT AS GOVERNOR.

AN Elephant was once appointed ruler of a forest. Now, it is well known that the race of elephants is endowed with great intelligence; but every family has its unworthy scion. Our Governor was as stout as the rest of his race are, but as foolish as the rest of his race are not. As to his character, he would not intentionally hurt a fly. Well, the worthy Governor becomes aware of a petition laid before him by the Sheep, stating that their skins are entirely torn off their backs by the Wolves.

"Oh, rogues!" cries the Elephant, "what a crime! Who gave you leave to plunder?

But the Wolves say,

"Allow us to explain, O father.   Did not you give us leave to take from the Sheep a trifling contribution* for our pelisses in winter?   It is only because they are stupid sheep that they cry out.   They have only a single fleece taken from each of them, but they grumble about giving even that!"

"Well, well," says the Elephant, "take care what you do.   I will not permit any one to commit injustice.   As it must be so, take a fleece from each of them.   But do not take from them a single hair besides."

He who has rank and power, but wants sense, however good his heart may be, is sure to do harm.

---

* *Obrok*—tne tax levied on the peasant by his master.

THE POOR MAN ENRICHED.

"IS IT worth while being rich, if one is never to eat or drink delicately, and to do nothing but heap up money? And to what end? We die, and then leave all behind. We only torment ourselves, and get a bad name. No; if riches had fallen to my share, not only roubles, but even thousands of them wouldn't have been grudged by me, so long as I could live sumptuously and luxuriously; and my feasts should have been talked about far and wide. Besides, I should have done good to others. To rich misers, their life is a kind of torment."

So reasoned a Poor Man with himself, lying on the bare boards in a wretched hovel. Suddenly, gliding to his side through a chink, there appeared—some say a wizard, others say the Evil One (most likely the latter, as the end of the story will show), and began to speak thus :

"You wish to be rich ; I have heard you say why. I am glad to help a friend, so here is a purse for you ; there is a ducat in it—no more. But, as soon as you have taken one coin out of it, you will find another in it all ready for you. So now, my friend, your growing rich depends entirely upon your own wishes. Take the purse, and freely supply yourself from it until your craving is satisfied. Only bear this in mind,—until you shall have flung the purse into the river, you are forbidden to spend a single ducat."

He spoke, and left the purse with the Poor Man. The Poor Man was almost beside himself for joy. But, as soon as he returned to his senses, he began to handle the purse; and with what result? Scarcely could he believe it was not a dream. He had hardly taken one ducat out, before another was already stirring in the purse. Our needy friend says to himself,

"I will shake out a heap of ducats. Then, to-morrow I shall be rich, and I will begin to live like a Sybarite."

But the next morning he had changed his mind.

"It's true," he says, "I am rich now. But who isn't glad to get hold of a good thing? and why shouldn't I become twice as rich? It surely wouldn't be laziness in me to spend another day over the purse. Here I have money for a mansion, an equipage, a country house. But if I might buy estates too, wouldn't it be stupid in me to lose such an opportunity? Yes, I will keep the wonderful purse. So be it: I will fast one day more. As to that, I shall always have time enough for luxurious living."

But what happens? A day goes by, and then a week, a month, a year. Our Poor Man has long ago lost all count of the ducats. Meanwhile, he eats scantily, and drinks scantily. Scarcely has the day begun to break before he is back at the old work. The day comes to an end; but, according to his calculations, something or other is still sure to be wanting. Sometimes he makes up his mind to throw

away the purse. But then his heart grows faint within him. He reaches the bank of the river, and—then turns back again.

"How can I possibly part with the purse," he says, "while it yields a stream of gold of its own accord?"

By this time our poor friend has grown grey, and thin, and as yellow as his own gold. He no more so much as thinks about luxury now. He has become faint and feeble; health and rest have utterly deserted him. But still with trembling hand he goes on taking ducats out of the purse. He takes, and takes; and how does it all end? On the bench on which he used to sit gloating over his wealth—on that very bench he dies, in the act of counting the last coins of his ninth million.

THE QUARTETTE.

THE tricksy Monkey, the Goat, the Ass, and bandy-legged Mishka the Bear, determine to play a quartette. They provide themselves with the necessary pieces of music—with two fiddles, and with an alto and a counter-bass. Then they sit down on a meadow under a lime-tree, prepared to enchant the world by their skill. They work away at their fiddlesticks with a will; and they make a noise, but there is no music in it.

"Stop, brothers, stop!" cries the Monkey, "wait a little! How can we get our music right? It's plain, you mustn't sit as you are. You, Mishka, with your counter-bass, face the alto. I will sit opposite the second fiddle. Then a different sort of music will begin: we shall set the very hills and forests dancing."

So they change places, and recommence; but the music is just as discordant as before.

" Stop a little," exclaims the Ass; " I have found out the secret. We shall be sure to play in tune if we sit in a row."

They follow its advice, and form in an orderly line. But the quartette is as unmusical as ever. Louder than before there arose among them squabbling and wrangling as to how they ought to be seated. It happened that a Nightingale came flying that way, attracted by their noise. At once they all intreat it to solve their difficulty.

" Be so kind," they say, " as to bear with us a little, in order that our quartette may come off properly. Music we have; instruments we have: tell us only how we ought to place ourselves."

But the Nightingale replies,

" To be a musician, one must have a quicker intelligence and a finer ear than you possess. You, my friends, may place yourselves just as you like, but you will never become musicians."

[Some writers say this fable alludes to the foundation, in March, 1811, of the "Society of Lovers of Russian Literature," which had four departments, and seemed more like a public office than a literary institution, and the members of which had places allotted to them according to their rank rather than to their talents. But Baron Korf says it refers to the disputes about places which arose among the firs Presidents of the four departments of the Imperial Council, at the time of its reconstruction, in the year 1810.]

"GOOD day, dear friend ; where do you come from ? "
"From the Museum, where I have spent three hours. I saw everything they have there, and examined it carefully. So much have I seen to astonish me, that, if you will believe me, I am neither strong enough nor clever enough to give you a full description of it. Upon my word it is a palace of wonders. How rich Nature is in invention ! What birds and beasts haven't I seen there ! What flies, butterflies, cockroaches, litt'e bits of beetles !—some like emeralds, others like coral. And what tiny cochineal insects ! Why, really, some of them are smaller than a pin's head."

" But did you see the elephant? What did you think it looked like ? I 'll be bound you felt as if you were looking at a mountain."

" Are you quite sure it 's there ? "

" Quite sure."

" Well, brother, you mustn't be too hard upon me; but, to tell the truth, I didn't remark the elephant."

[Bulgarine states that Krilof wrote this fable in allusion to the remark of some one, perhaps Prince Viazemsky, that each of the three great fabulists, La Fontaine, Khemnitser, and Dmitrief, bore the name of Ivan,—thus omitting all notice of Ivan Krilof. But the story does not seem to rest on any substantial authority, and it is entirely out of keeping with all the other anecdotes about Krilof, who was remarkably modest and unpretentious.]

THE COOK AND THE CAT.

A CERTAIN Cook, rather more educated than his fellows,
went from his kitchen one day to a neighbouring tavern
—he was of a serious turn of mind, and on that day he celebrated the anniversary of a friend's death—leaving a Cat at
home, to guard his viands from the mice. On his return, what
does he see? The floor strewed with fragments of a pie, and
Vaska the Cat crouching in a corner behind a vinegar-barrel,
purring with satisfaction, and busily engaged in disposing of
a chicken.

"Ah, glutton! ah, evil-doer!" exclaims the reproachful
Cook. "Are you not ashamed of being seen by these walls,

let alone living witnesses? What! be an honourable Cat up to this time—one who might be pointed out as a model of discretion! And now, ah me! how great a disgrace! Now all the neighbours will say, 'The cat Vaska is a rogue; the cat Vaska is a thief. Vaska must not be admitted into the kitchen, not even into the courtyard, any more than a ravenous wolf into the sheepfold. He is utterly corrupt; he is a pest, the plague of the neighbourhood.'"

Thus did our orator, letting loose the current of his words, lecture away without stopping. But what was the result? While he was delivering his discourse, Vaska the Cat ate up the whole of the chicken.

I would advise some cooks to inscribe these words on their walls : " Don't waste time in useless speech, when it is action that is needed."

THE MUSICIANS.

A CERTAIN man invited a neighbour to dinner, not without an ulterior purpose. He was fond of music, and he entrapped his neighbour into his house to listen to his choir. The honest fellows began to sing, each on his own account, and each with all his might. The guest's ears began to split, and his head to turn.

"Have pity on me!" he exclaimed, in amazement. "What can any one like in all this? Why, your choristers bawl like madmen."

"It's quite true," replied the host, with feeling. "They do flay one's ears just a trifle. But, on the other hand, they are all of irreproachable behaviour, and they never touch a drop of intoxicating liquor."

But, I say, in my opinion you had better drink a little, if needs be: only take care to understand your business thoroughly.

THE PEASANT AND THE LABOURER.

AN old Peasant and a Labourer were going home through
the forest to the village one evening, in the time of
the hay-harvest, when they suddenly found themselves face
to face with a bear. Scarcely had the Peasant time to utter
a cry when the bear was upon him; it threw him down,
rolled him over, made his bones crack again, and began
looking about for a soft spot at which to commence its
meal. Death draws near to the old man.

"Stefan, my kinsman, my dear friend, do not desert me!"
he cries, from under the bear, to the Labourer.

Then Stefan, putting forth all his strength like a new

4

Hercules, splits the bear's head in two with his axe, and drives his pitchfork into its bowels. The bear howls, and falls dying. Our bear expires.

The danger having vanished, the Peasant gets up, and soundly scolds the Labourer. Our poor Stefan is astounded.

"Pardon me, what have I done?"

"What have you done, you blockhead? I'd like to know what you are so absurdly pleased about; why, you've gone and struck the bear in such a manner that you've utterly ruined his fur!"

THE BEAR AMONG THE BEES.

THE beasts elected the Bear, one spring, Inspector of
the Beehives. They might, it is true, have chosen a
more trustworthy animal, seeing that the Bear is passionately
fond of honey. The matter was one to be regretted; but
who can expect wisdom from beasts? Every other solicitor
for the post of Hive Inspector they sent away with a refusal,
and finally, as if by way of pleasantry, the Bear made his
appearance in that capacity. But harm soon came of the
appointment for our Bear carried off all the honey into his
den. The theft was found out, an alarm was sounded, and
legal proceedings were taken in due form. Eventually, the

4—2

Bear was dismissed from his office, and the old rogue was sentenced to lie in his den all the winter.

The Court decided, ratified, and countersigned; but, in spite of all this, it did not return the honey. As for Mishka, he didn't pay the slightest attention to the affair. Bidding the world farewell for a season, he betook himself to his warm den. There he sucks his honeyed paw, and waits till fair weather invites him to a fresh cruise.

[At the time when Krilof wrote, extortion and corruption were scandalously rife in Russia. The Government strove hard to put down the extortioners, and the Press did all that it could, in its fettered condition, to aid in so good a cause. But, in spite of all that could be done, the evil went on flourishing. As soon as Alexander I. came to the throne, he issued an edict against exactions of every kind; and in 1809, when the great abuses in the Commissariat Department had been brought to light, he renewed the old ukases of Peter the Great and Catherine II. The first, published in 1714, orders that all persons convicted of extorting money and taking bribes shall undergo severe corporal punishment, shall forfeit all their property, and shall be " treated as rascals, and turned out of the list of honest people." The second, of the date of 1763, ordains that they shall be " not only turned out of the ranks of honest people, but eliminated from the entire human race." But, notwithstanding all these energetic declarations, the forbidden practices remained unchecked; and, to the end of Alexander's reign, each year saw a new edict issued on the subject. In 1816, especially, a vigorous attempt was made to produce a reform, and a rescript was addressed to the Minister of Justice, bidding him see that the law courts should be rendered the means of maintaining right, not of confirming wrong ; and that assistance should be given to the weak and needy in their appeals against oppression. But it too often occurred that, when some great man had been detected in robbing the poor, the only punishment he underwent was a nominal banishment to his estates, where he enjoyed, like the Bear, the fruits of his villainy, and waited till the temporary ill wind should have blown over.]

THE HORSE AND THE DOG.

A DOG and a Horse, which served the same peasant, began to discuss each other's merits, one day.

"How grand we are, to be sure!" says Barbos. "I shouldn't be sorry if they were to turn you out of the farm-yard. A noble service, indeed, to plough or to draw a cart! And I've never heard of any other proof of your merit. How can you possibly compare yourself with me? I rest neither by day nor by night. In the daytime I watch the cattle in the meadows; by night I guard the house."

"Quite true," replied the Horse. "What you say is perfectly correct. Only remember that, if it weren't for my ploughing, you wouldn't have anything at all to guard here."

"NEIGHBOUR, light of my eyes! do eat a little more."
"Dear neighbour, I am full to the throat."

"No matter; just a little plateful. Believe me, the soup is cooked gloriously."

"But I've had three platefuls already."

"Well, what does that matter? If you like it and it does you good, why not eat it all up? What a soup it is! How rich! It looks as if it had been sprinkled over with amber. Here is bream; there is a lump of sterlet. Take a little more, dear, kind friend. Just another spoonful! Wife, come and intreat him."

Thus does Demian feast his neighbour Phocas, not giving him a moment's breathing-time. Phocas feels the moisture trickling down his forehead; still he takes one more plateful, attacks it with all the strength he has left, and somehow manages to swallow the whole of it.

"That's the sort of friend I like!" cries Demian. "I can't bear people who require pressing. But now, dear friend, take just one little plateful more!"

But, on hearing this, our poor Phocas, much as he liked fish soup, catching hold of his cap and sash, runs away home

without looking behind him.   Nor from that day to this has
he crossed Demian's threshold.

[There was a meeting one day, at the house of the poet
Derjavine, of the members of the "Society of the Lovers of
Russian Literature."   Krilof had promised to attend, and to
read one of his new and, as yet, unpublished fables ; but he
did not appear till very late.   When he arrived, some one was
reading an exceeedingly long poem, which went on and on
until the audience was utterly worn out.   At last, however,
it came to an end.   Then Krilof was asked to read his poem ;
so he put his hand in his pocket, produced a piece of paper,
and read " Demian's Fish Soup."   It is easy to imagine how
thoroughly it was appreciated by an audience which had just
been suffering tortures at the hands of a literary Demian—
one of those authors who, when they have once secured a
hearing, never know when it is time to leave off.]

THE WOLVES AND THE SHEEP.

THE Sheep could not live in peace on account of the Wolves, and the evil increased to such a pitch, that at last the rulers of the beasts had to take vigorous steps towards interfering and saving the victims. With that intent a council was summoned. The majority of its members, it is true, were Wolves; but then all Wolves are not badly spoken of. There have been Wolves known, and that often (such instances are never forgotten), to have walked past a flock quite peacefully—when completely gorged. So why should not Wolves have seats in the council? Although it was necessary to protect the Sheep, yet there was no reason for utterly suppressing the Wolves.

Well, the meeting took place in the thick wood. They pondered, considered, harangued, and at last framed a decree. Here you have it, word for word :—" As soon as a Wolf shall have disturbed a flock, and shall have begun to worry a Sheep, then the Sheep shall be allowed, without respect to persons, to seize it by the scruff of the neck, to carry it into the nearest thicket or wood, and there to bring it before the court."

This law is everything that can be desired. Only, I have remarked, up to the present day, that although the Wolves are not to be allowed to worry with impunity, yet in all cases, whether the Sheep be plaintiff or defendant, the Wolf is always sure, in spite of all opposition, to carry off the Sheep into the forest.

THE MAN AND HIS SHADOW.

THERE was a certain original who must needs desire to catch his own Shadow. He makes a step or two towards it, but it moves away before him. He quickens his pace; it does the same. At last he takes to running; but the quicker he goes, the quicker runs the Shadow also, utterly refusing to give itself up, just as if it had been a treasure. But see! our eccentric friend suddenly turns round, and walks away from it. And presently he looks behind him; the Shadow runs after him now.

Ladies fair, I have often observed——what do you suppose?—no, no; I assure you I am not going to speak about you——that Fortune treats us in a similar way. One man tries with all his might to seize the goddess, and only loses his time and his trouble. Another seems, to all appearance, to be running out of her sight; but, no: she herself takes a pleasure in pursuing him.

A WOLF, which had begun to accustom its Cub to support itself by its father's profession, sent it one day to prowl about the skirts of the wood. At the same time it ordered it to give all its attention to seeing whether it would not be possible, even at the cost of sinning a little, for them both to make their breakfast or dinner at the expense of some shepherd or other. The pupil returns home, and says—

"Come along, quick! Our dinner awaits us : nothing could possibly be safer. There are sheep feeding at the foot of yon hill, each one fatter than the other. We have only to choose which to carry off and eat ; and the flock is so large that it would be difficult to count it over again——"

"Wait a minute," says the Wolf. "First of all I must know what sort of a man the shepherd of this flock is.

"It is said that he is a good one—painstaking and intelligent. But I went round the flock on all sides, and examined the dogs : they are not at all fat, and seem to be spiritless and indolent."

"This description," says the old Wolf, "does not greatly attract me to the flock. For, decidedly, if the shepherd is good, he will not keep bad dogs about him.   One might very soon get into trouble there.   But come with me : I will take you to a flock where we shall be in less danger of losing our skins.   Over that flock it is true that a great many dogs watch ; but the shepherd is himself a fool.   And where the shepherd is a fool, there the dogs too are of little worth."

THE DANCING FISH.

HAVING waters as well as woods in his dominions, the Lion called the beasts together to a council, to consider who should be appointed governor of the Fish. They gave their votes in the usual manner, and the Fox was chosen. Well, the Fox sat in the governor's seat, and visibly waxed fat. He had a Moujik as friend, kinsman, and gossip, and the two used to lay their heads together. The Fox conducted business and pronounced legal decisions on the shore; and meantime his gossip angled after the Fish, and, like a trusty, comrade, shared what he caught with his friend.

But rogues do not always succeed. The Lion somehow

grew suspicious, from rumours it heard, that the scales had
been falsified in its law courts; so, having found a leisure
time, it determined to investigate the state of its dominions.

Having gone to the shore, it found that the good gossip
had caught some fish, and had kindled a fire by the river-
side, intending to feast on them with his comrade. The
poor fish were bounding into the air to get away from the
heat, each one to the best of its power : each one, seeing its
end close at hand, flung itself about, gaping at the Moujik.

"Who are you, and what are you doing?" angrily asked
the Lion.

"Great king!" answers the chief rogue—the Fox always
has a trick in reserve—"great king! this is my chief secretary here, who is esteemed for his probity by all the nation ;
and these are carp, all inhabitants of the waters. We have
all come here to congratulate you, our good king, on your
arrival."

"Well, how is justice dispensed here? Is your district
content?"

"Great king! here they do not merely live; they are in
Paradise. If only your royal life may be prolonged!" (All
this time the fish were leaping about in the pan.)

"But tell me," said the Lion, "why do they fling themselves about topsy-turvy in this manner?"

"O wise Lion," replied the Fox, "they are dancing for
joy at seeing you."

Not being able to stand such a manifest fiction as this,
the Lion, in order that there should be some music for its

subjects to dance to, made the secretary and the governor both sing out under its claws.

[This fable, as originally written by Krilof, ended as follows :

" O wise Lion," replied the Fox, " they are dancing for joy at seeing you." Then the Lion, tapping the Starost kindly on the breast, proceeded on his journey.

But the censor objected that this seemed like a reflection on the Emperor Alexander, who was then—it was in the year 1824—making what was destined to be his last journey through Russia. Krilof at first refused to make any alteration ; but eventually he modified the fable, and added the lines with which it now concludes.

There is a tradition that, during one of his travels in the interior, the Emperor Alexander I. spent a night, in some city or other, in the governor's house. The next morning, just as he was on the point of continuing his journey, he happened to look out of window, and saw a great crowd collected in front of the house. The governor, being asked what was the cause of it, replied that it was a deputation of the inhabitants, who wished to thank the Emperor for the happy lives they led. As the Emperor was in a hurry to get away, he declined to receive the deputation, and drove off.

Afterwards it turned out that the people had come to complain of their governor, who oppressed them terribly.]

THE PIKE.

AN appeal to justice was made against the Pike, on the ground that it had rendered the pond uninhabitable. A whole cart-load of proofs were tendered as evidence; and the culprit, as was beseeming, was brought into court in a large tub. The judges were assembled not far off, having been set to graze in a neighbouring field. Their names are still preserved in the archives. There were two Donkeys, a couple of old Horses, and two or three Goats. The Fox also was added to their number, as assessor, in order that the business might be carried on under competent supervision.

Now, popular report said that the Pike used to supply the table of the Fox with fish. However this might be, there was no partiality among the judges; and it must also be stated that it was impossible to conceal the Pike's roguery in the affair in question. So there was no help for it. Sentence was passed, condemning the Pike to an ignominious punishment. In order to frighten others, it was to be hung from a tree.

"Respected judges," thus did the Fox begin to speak, "hanging is a trifle. I should have liked to have sentenced the culprit to such a punishment as has never been seen here among us. In order that rogues may in future live in fear, and run a terrible risk, I would drown it in the river."

"Excellent!" cry the judges, and unanimously accept the proposition.

So the Pike was flung—into the river.

THE GEESE.

A PEASANT, with a long rod in his hand, was driving
some Geese to a town where they were to be sold;
and, to tell the truth, he did not treat them over-politely. In
hopes of making a good bargain, he was hastening on so as
not to lose the market-day (and when gain is concerned,
geese and men alike are apt to suffer).   I do not blame the
peasant; but the Geese talked about him in a different
spirit, and, whenever they met any passers-by, abused him
to them in such terms as these:

"Is it possible to find any Geese more unfortunate than
we are? This Moujik harasses us so terribly, and chases us

about just as if we were common Geese.   The ignoramus
does not know that he ought to pay us reverence, seeing
that we are the noble descendants of those geese to whom
Rome was once indebted for her salvation, and in whose
honour even feast-days were specially appointed there."

"And do you want to have honour paid you on that
account?" a passer-by asked them.

" Why, our ancestors——"

" I know that—I have read all about it ; but I want to
know this—of what use have you been yourselves?"

" Why, our ancestors saved Rome !"

" Quite so ; but what have you done?"

" We?   Nothing."

" Then what merit is there in you?   Let your ancestors
rest in peace—they justly received honourable reward ; but
you, my friends, are only fit to be roasted !"

It would be easy to make this fable still more intelligible ;
but I am afraid of irritating the Geese.

THE LION AND THE PANTHER.

ONCE on a time, in ancient days, the Lion maintained a very long contest with the Panther about certain disputed forests, valleys, and caves. To go to law about their rights—this was not in accordance with their characters; for, in matters relating to law, the strong are often blind. For such affairs they have their own rule,—"Who conquers is right." But at last, that they might not eternally squabble, with claws ever becoming more blunt, our heroes determined to submit their dispute to law. Their intention was to put an end to their fighting, to settle all hostilities, and then, as is customary, to conclude a peace which should last uninterrupted—until the next quarrel.

"Let us each choose a secretary at once," proposes the Panther to the Lion, "and decide according as the two secretaries shall advise. I, for instance, will choose the Cat. It is not a very good-looking little animal; but, then, its conscience is clear. But do you, for your part, nominate the Ass, for it belongs to a distinguished order in the state; and, to tell the truth, you will have in it a very enviable beast. Trust me as a friend in this. All your court and council together are scarcely worth its hoof. Let us accept whatever arrangements it and my Cat may make."

And the Lion sanctioned the first part of the Panther's scheme without opposition ; only he chose the Fox, instead of the Ass, to represent him in the discussion, saying to himself, after so doing,

"Truly, there is but little good to be gained from him whom an enemy recommends."

THE COMB.

A LOVING mother bought a good strong Comb to keep her boy's hair in order. The child never let his new present go out of his hands. Whether playing or learning his alphabet, he was always lovingly passing his Comb through the twining curls of his waving golden hair, soft as fine flax. And what a Comb it was! Not only did it not pull out his hair, but it never even got caught in it; so smoothly and easily did it glide through his locks. It was a priceless Comb in the eyes of the child. But at last it happened, one day, that the Comb was mislaid. Our boy went playing and romping about, until he got his hair into a regular tangle. Scarcely had the nurse touched it, when he began to howl,

"Where is my Comb?"

At last it was found; but when they tried to pass it through his locks, it could not be moved either backwards or forwards: all it did was to pull his hair out by the roots, so as to bring the tears into his eyes.

"How wicked you are, you bad Comb!" cries the boy.

But the Comb replies,

"My dear, I am what I always was; only your hair has become tangled."

Whereupon our young friend, giving way to rage and vexation, flings his Comb into the river. And now the Naiads comb their hair with it.

In my time I have often seen men behave in a like manner towards the truth. As long as we have a clear conscience, truth is agreeable to us, we hold it sacred, we listen to it and obey it; but as soon as a man has begun to do violence to his conscience, the truth becomes alien to his ears. Then every one resembles the boy who did not like to have his hair combed after it had got into a tangle.

THE AUTHOR AND THE ROBBER.

IN the gloomy realm of shadows, two sinners appeared
before the judges for sentence at the very same time.
The one was a Robber, who used to extract tribute on the
highway, and who had at last come to the gallows; the other
an Author, covered with glory, who had infused a subtle poison
into his works, had promoted atheism, and had preached
immorality, being, like the Siren, sweet-voiced, and, like the
Siren, dangerous. In Hades judical ceremonies are brief;
there are no useless delays. Sentence was pronounced immediately. Two huge iron cauldrons were suspended in the
air by two tremendous iron chains; in each of these one of
the sinners was placed. Under the Robber a great pile of
wood was heaped up, and then one of the Furies herself set
it on fire, kindling such a terrible flame, that the very stone in
the roof of the infernal halls began to crack. The Author's
sentence did not seem to be a severe one. Under him, at first,
a little fire scarcely glowed; but, the longer it burned, the
larger it became.

Centuries have now gone by, but the fire has not gone
out. Beneath the Robber the flame has long ago been extinguished; beneath the Author it grows hourly worse and
worse. Seeing that there is no mitigation of his torments,

the writer at last cries out amidst them that there is no justice among the gods; that he had filled the world with his renown; and that, if he had written a little too freely, he had been punished too much for it ; and that he did not think he had sinned more than the Robber.   Then before him, in all her ornaments, with snakes hissing amid her hair, and with bloody scourges in her hands, appeared one of the three Infernal Sisters.

"Wretch !" she exclaims, "dost thou upbraid Providence? Dost thou compare thyself with this robber?   His crime is as nothing compared with thine.   Only as long as he lived did his cruelty and lawlessness render him hurtful.   But thou —long ago have thy bones turned to dust, yet the sun never rises without bringing to light fresh evils of which thou art the cause.   The poison of thy writings not only does not weaken, but, spreading abroad, it becomes more malignant as years roll by.   Look there !" and for a moment she enables him to look upon the world ; "behold the crimes, the misery, of which thou art the cause.   Look at those children who have brought shame upon their families, who have reduced their parents to despair.   By whom were their heads and hearts corrupted ?   By thee.   Who strove to rend asunder the bonds of society, ridiculing as childish follies all ideas of the sanctity of marriage and the right of authority and law, and rendering them responsible for all human misfortunes ? Thou art the man !   Didst thou not dignify unbelief with the name of enlightenment ?   Didst thou not place vice and passion in the most charming and alluring of lights ?   And now look!—a whole country, perverted by thy teaching, is full of murder and robbery, of strife and rebellion, and is being led onwards by thee to ruin. For every drop of that country's tears and blood thou art to blame. And now dost thou dare to hurl thy blasphemies against the gods? How much evil have thy books yet to bring upon the world? Continue, then, to suffer; for here the measure of thy punishment shall be according to thy deserts." Thus spoke the angry Fury, and slammed down the cover on the cauldron.

[There seems to be little doubt that Krilof was thinking of Voltaire when he wrote this somewhat violent diatribe. "We prefer to believe," says the French translator of Krilof, in a note on this passage, "that, in spite of his errors, the apostle of universal toleration, the ardent promoter of so many useful and humane reforms, the zealous defender of so many innocent persons, will find less severity in his real Judge than he finds here in the Minos of the fable."]

THE HIND AND THE DERVISH.

A YOUNG Hind, bereft of her much-loved fawns, and still having her udders full of milk, found two young wolves deserted in a forest, and immediately began to fulfil the sacred duty of a mother towards them, feeding them with her milk. A Dervish, who inhabited the same forest, astonished at this proceeding of hers, cried out—

"Imprudent creature that thou art! On what kind of animal art thou conferring thy milk? on what art thou wasting thy affections? Is it possible that thou canst expect gratitude from such as they are? Or is it that thou dost not know their evil nature? Some day, perhaps, it will be thy blood that they will drink."

"It may be so, indeed," replied the Hind; "but I did not think, nor do I wish to think, of that. It is only as a mother that I care to feel just now; and my milk would have been a burden to me if I had not given suck to these little ones."

Thus genuine charity does good without thinking of recompense. To the really benevolent, their abundance would be burdensome if they could not share it with those who are in want.

CANINE FRIENDSHIP.

UNDER a kitchen window lay Barbos and Polkan, basking in the sunshine. It would have been more fitting in them to have been guarding the house at the gate in front of the courtyard. But they had eaten till they were satiated, and, besides, polite dogs do not bark at any one in the daytime. So they indulged in a discussion about all sorts of things—about their doggish service, about good and evil, and finally about friendship.

"What," says Polkan, "can be pleasanter than to live heart to heart with a friend?—in everything to offer mutual service; not to sleep or eat without one's friend, and to defend his

body with all one's force; finally, for friends to look into one
another's eyes, and each to think that only a fortunate hour
in which he could please or amuse his friend, and to place
all his own happiness in his friend's good fortune! Suppose,
for instance, you and I were to contract such a friendship.
I venture to say, we should not be able to tell how quickly
time was flying."

"That is true. So be it," replies Barbos. "Long has it
been grievous to me, my dear Polkan, that we, who are dogs
of the same yard, cannot spend a single day without quarrelling: and why is it? Thanks to our master, we are
neither closely pent nor scantily fed. Besides, it really is
scandalous. From the earliest times the dog has been the
type of friendship; yet you scarcely ever see any more friendship among dogs than among men."

"Let us make manifest an instance of it to our own times,"
says Polkan.

"Your paw!"

"There it is."

Straightway the new friends begin to caress and fondle
each other. They know not, in their raptures, to what to liken
themselves.

"My Orestes!"

"My Pylades!"

"Away with all quarrels, all envy, all malice!"

Unluckily, at this moment the cook tosses a bone out of the
kitchen. Our new friends fling themselves upon it furiously.
What has become of their harmonious alliance? Orestes and

Pylades seize each other by the throat, so that their hair goes flying to the winds, and even torrents of water will scarcely separate them.

The world is full of such friendships. One would not be far wrong if one said of friends, as they are now-a-days, that they are almost all alike in respect to their friendship. To listen to them, you would imagine they were perfectly unanimous. But just throw them a bone; they will behave exactly like our dogs.*

---

* Kenevich says that this fable, which appeared in May, 1815, was suggested by the proceedings of the Congress of Vienna.

THE CUCKOO AND THE COCK.

"HOW proudly and sonorously you sing, my dear Cock!"

"But you, dear Cuckoo, my light, how smoothly flows your long-drawn-out note! There is no such singer in all the rest of our forest."

"To you, my dear gossip, I could listen for ever."

"And as for you, my beauty, I swear that, when you are silent, I scarcely know how to wait till you begin again. Where do you get such a voice from?—so clear, so soft, and so high! But no doubt you were always like that; not very large in stature, but in song—a regular nightingale."

"Thanks, gossip. As for you, I declare, on my conscience, you sing better than the birds in the garden of Eden. For a proof of this, I appeal to public opinion."

At this moment a Sparrow, which had overheard their conversation, said to them,

"You may go on praising one another till you are hoarse, my friends; but your music is utterly worthless."

Why was it that, not being afraid to sin, the Cuckoo praised the Cock? Simply because the Cock praised the Cuckoo.*

* This is said to allude to the perpetual interchange of compliments which used to take place between the editors of the "Northern Bee"—Grech and Bulgarine.

THE PEASANTS AND THE RIVER.

SOME Peasants, who had been driven out of all patience by the ruin which the brooks and rivulets had brought upon them by their overflowing, set out to seek redress from the River into which those streams fell. And, indeed, there was much reason for denouncing them. They had torn away the seed from the newly-sown fields, they had overthrown and washed away mills, and it was impossible to count the cattle they had drowned. But the River flows so gently, though indeed proudly: on its banks great cities stand, and no one ever hears such tricks laid to its charge. So, doubtless, it will put a check upon these streams.

Thus did the Peasants reason among themselves. But what happened? When they had drawn near to the banks of the River, and looked out upon its surface, they saw that its stream was bearing along half of their missing property. The Peasants, without beginning a fruitless complaint, only gazed on the waters for awhile. Then, after looking in each other's faces, and shaking their heads, they returned home; and as they went, they said,

" Why should we waste our time? You 'll never get any redress for what the children have stolen, so long as their parents go halves with them in the spoil."

[The best comment upon this fable is that supplied by Trutofsky's illustration of it. A number of peasants have come to lay before the district Ispravnik, or officer of rural police, a complaint against some of their petty oppressors. But, on arriving near the Ispravnik's house, they see that worthy standing in his verandah, benignantly smiling on the two men they have come to complain of, who are offering him a variety of presents, all of which the peasants recognise as having formerly belonged to themselves. Horrified at the sight, they are evidently about to retire without laying their case before such a judge.]

AN empty Bag long lay neglected on the ground, in the corner of an antechamber, the lowest menials of the house often using it as a mat to rub their shoes upon. But suddenly our Bag was turned to honourable account, and filled full of ducats. In an iron-bound coffer it now lies in security. Its master caresses it with his own hand, and takes such care of it that not a breath of wind is able to ruffle it; no fly dares to light upon it. Besides this, the whole town becomes well acquainted with the Bag. If a friend comes to visit its master, he willingly begins to say pleasant things about the Bag. Whenever it is opened, every one smiles sweetly upon it; and whoever sits down by its side is sure to pat it or stroke it affectionately, seeing that it is universally respected. The Bag begins to be puffed up, to make much of itself, to air its cleverness. It begins to chatter and to give utterance to nonsense, discussing and criticising everything : "This is not so," and "That man is a fool," or "That affair will turn out badly." Every one gives it his entire attention, listening with open mouth, although it talks nonsense enough to make their ears tingle. But, unfortunately, men have this weakness, that they are sure to admire whatever a Bag says, so long as it is full of ducats.

6—2

But did the Bag long enjoy honour?—did its reputation for cleverness last, and was it long the object of endearment? Only until its last ducat had been taken out of it : then it was flung out of doors, and nothing more was ever heard of it.

[To this Bag Krilof compares many of the wealthy brandy-tax farmers.* Some of them, he says, were once mere waiters in petty taverns, but have now grown rich, and assumed airs of importance. "A million is a great fact. Only, friends, don't be too proud. Shall I whisper the truth to you? God grant you may not get ruined! For, if you do, the same fate will befall you that befell the Bag."]

---

* Contractors who farmed the tax on spirits, and made colossal fortunes, supplying the peasants with the worst of liquors, and getting as much as they could out of them. The whole system has now been altered, and this class of contractors no longer exists.

FORTUNE AND THE BEGGAR.

A WRETCHED Beggar, carrying a ragged old wallet, was creeping along from house to house; and, as he grumbled at his lot, he kept wondering that folks who lived in rich apartments, and were up to their throats in money and in the sweets of indulgence, should be always unsatisfied, however full their pockets might be, and that they should go so far as often to lose all they have, while unreasonably craving for, and laying their hands on, new riches. "Here, for instance," he says, "the former master of this house succeeded in trading prosperously, and made himself enormously rich by commerce. But then, instead of stopping, and handing over his business to another, and spending the rest of his years in peace, he took to equipping ships for the sea in the spring. He expected to get mountains of gold ; but the ships were smashed, and his treasures were swallowed up by the waves. Now they all lie at the bottom of the sea, and he has found his riches melt away like those in dreams. Another man became one of the farmers of the spirit-tax, and so gained a million. That was a trifle : he wanted to double it. So he plunged up to his ears in speculations, and was utterly ruined. In short, instances of this are countless. And quite right too : a man should use discretion."

At this moment Fortune suddenly appeared to the Beggar, and said, " Listen ! I have long wished to help you. Here is a lot of ducats I have found. Hold out your wallet, and I will fill it with them ; but only on this condition :—All shall be gold that falls into the wallet ; but if any of it falls out of the wallet to the ground, it shall all become dust. Consider this well. I have warned you beforehand. I shall keep strictly to my compact. Your wallet is old ; don't overload it beyond its powers."

Our Beggar is almost too overjoyed to breathe. He scarcely feels the ground beneath his feet. He opens his wallet, and with generous hand a golden stream of ducats is poured into it. The wallet soon becomes rather heavy.

" Is that enough ?"

" Not yet."

" Isn't it cracking ?"

" Never fear."

" Consider, you 're quite a Crœsus."

" Just a little more ; just add a handful."

" There, it 's full. Take care : the wallet is going to burst."

" Just a little bit more."

But at that moment the wallet split ; the treasure fell through, and turned to dust; and Fortune disappeared. The Beggar had nothing but his empty wallet, and remained as poor as before.

THE Eagle promoted a Cuckoo to the rank of a Nightingale. The Cuckoo, proud of its new position, seated itself proudly on an aspen, and began to exhibit its musical talents. After a time, it looks round. All the birds are flying away, some laughing at it, others abusing it. Our Cuckoo grows angry, and hastens to the Eagle with a complaint against the birds.

"Have pity on me!" it says. "According to your command, I have been appointed Nightingale to these woods, and yet the birds dare to laugh at my singing."

"My friend," answers the Eagle, "I am a king, but I am not God. It is impossible for me to remedy the cause of your complaint. I can order a Cuckoo to be styled a Nightingale; but to make a Nightingale out of a Cuckoo—that I cannot do."

THE ASS.

A PEASANT had an Ass which seemed to behave itself
so discreetly that he could not praise it too highly.
But, in order that it might not get lost in the forest, our
peasant tied a bell round its neck. On this our Ass, who
had evidently heard a great deal of talk about decorations,
became puffed up, began to grow proud and conceited, and
looked upon itself as a very important gentleman. But its
new rank proved ruinous to the Ass, poor thing!—a fact
which may serve as a lesson for others besides asses. I ought
to tell you beforehand that the Ass was never over-honest;

but until it got its bell everything went smoothly with it. If it made its way into a field of rye or oats, or into a garden, it ate what it wanted, and then got out again quietly. But now it is a very different story with him. Whenever our illustrious gentleman trespasses, the bell which now adorns his neck goes with him, and rings an incessant peal. Every-one looks out to see what it is. Here, one man, seizing a bludgeon, drives our poor beast out of his rye-field or his garden ; and there, another, who owns a field of oats, no sooner hears the sound of the bell, than he catches up a stake, and begins thrashing the unfortunate animal's flanks. So that by the autumn our poor grandee is half dead : the Ass has nothing left but skin and bone.*

In the same way among men, also, rank proves injurious to rogues. As long as a rogue's position is humble, he is not remarked. But a lofty rank is, to a rogue, as it were a bell round his neck. Its noise is loud, and may be heard afar off.

---

* There is a good deal of resemblance between this Ass and the Dog in one of Æsop's fables.

THE LANDLORD AND THE MICE.

A CERTAIN Merchant built a magazine, in which he stored away his stock of edibles; and, in order that the mice should not damage them, he instituted a police of cats. And now the Merchant lives in peace. His stores are patrolled day and night, and all goes well. Unfortunately, an unexpected contingency occurs. One of the guardians proves himself a thief. Among cats, as with us (who knows it not?), the police are not faultless. But then, instead of detecting and punishing the thief, and sparing the honest servant, our landlord orders all his cats to be whipped. As soon as they hear this ingenious sentence, honest and guilty alike, they all run out of the house as quickly as possible : our landlord remains catless. This is just what the mice have been hoping and longing for. They enter the stores as soon as the cats have left, and in two or three weeks they contrive to eat up the whole of their contents.

[This fable, printed in 1811, probably alludes to the consequences of the wholesale punishment inflicted on the officials of the Commissariat and Victualling Departments during the war with France. They were disgraced in a body, and their uniforms were taken from them. The result was, that numbers of them retired from the service, rather than put up with such a slight. Krilof was interested in the matter; for the sister of one of his best friends was married to the General-Provision-Master.]

THE PEASANT AND THE SHEEP.

A PEASANT summoned a Sheep into court, charging the poor thing with a criminal offence. The judge was—the Fox. The case got into full swing immediately. Plaintiff and defendant were equally adjured to state, point by point, and without both speaking at once, how the affair took place, and in what their proofs consisted.

Says the Peasant: "On such and such a day, I missed two of my fowls early in the morning. Nothing was left of them but bones and feathers. And no one had been in the yard but the Sheep." Then the Sheep depones that it was fast asleep all the night in question; and it calls all its neighbours to testify that they had never known it guilty either of theft or of any roguery; and, besides this, it states that it never touches flesh-meat.

Here is the Fox's decision, word for word:

"The explanation of the Sheep cannot under any circumstances be accepted. For all rogues are notoriously clever at concealing their real designs; and it appears manifest, on due inquiry, that on the aforesaid night the Sheep was not separated from the fowls; and fowls are exceedingly savoury, and opportunity favoured it. Therefore I decide, according to my conscience, that it is impossible that the Sheep could have forborne to eat the fowls; and accordingly the Sheep shall be put to death, and its carcase shall be given to the court, and its fleece shall be taken by the plaintiff."

THE RAZORS.

AS I was travelling, one day, I fell in with an acquaintance, and we spent the night in the same bed-room. As soon as I awake next morning, what do I hear? My friend is evidently in trouble. The night before, we had both gone to bed merry and free from care; but now my friend is entirely changed: he groans, he sighs, he mutters words of complaining.

"What is the matter, my friend?" I cry. "You're not ill, I hope."

"Oh, no," he replies; "but I'm shaving."

"What! is that all?" I exclaim; and thereupon I get up

and look at him.   The strange fellow is making faces at
himself in the looking-glass, with tears in his eyes, and looking
as agonized all the time as if he were expecting to be flayed
alive.   When I had at last discovered the cause of such suf-
ferings, I say to him, " It's no wonder, and it's entirely your
own fault that you are so much hurt.   Just look at those
things of yours.   They are more like carving-knives than
razors : as to shaving with them, that is impossible.   All you
can do is to scrape yourself painfully with them."

" I must allow, brother," he replies, " that the razors are
excessively blunt ; how can I help knowing that ?   I 'm not
such a fool as all that.   But I never use sharp ones, for fear
of cutting myself."

" But I venture to assure you, my friend, that you will cut
yourself much sooner with a blunt razor.   With a sharp one
you will shave yourself twice as safely ; only you must know
how to use it properly."

Are there not many, though they would be ashamed to
own it, who are afraid of clever people, and are more ready
to have fools about them ?

THE MONKEY AND THE MIRROR.

A MONKEY, which saw its image one day in a mirror, gave a Bear a slight push with its foot, and said, "Only look, my dear gossip, what a hideous creature that is! What grimaces it makes! How it skips about! I should hang myself from vexation if I were at all like that. But, if we must tell the truth, are there not in the number of our friends five or six such grimacers?"

"Why take the trouble to count up your friends? Would it not be better to take a look at yourself?" answered the Bear.

But Mishka's advice was only thrown away uselessly.

There are plenty of examples of this in the world. No one is ready to recognise himself in a satire. I remarked that only yesterday. We all know that Clement's hands are not clean. Every one charges Clement with taking bribes; but he shakes his head with secret horror when he thinks of Peter's unjust proceedings.

THE ELEPHANT IN FAVOUR.

ONCE upon a time, the Elephant stood high in the good graces of the Lion. The forest immediately began to talk about the matter, and, as usual, many guesses were made as to the means by which the Elephant had gained such favour.

"It is no beauty," say the beasts to each other, "and it is not amusing. And what habits it has! what manners!"

Says the Fox, whisking about his brush, "If it had possessed such a bushy tail as mine, I should not have wondered."

"Or, sister," says the Bear, "if it had got into favour on account of claws, no one would have found the matter at all extraordinary; but it has no claws at all, as we all know well."

"Isn't it its tusks that have got it into favour?" thus the Ox broke in upon their conversation. "Haven't they, perhaps, been mistaken for horns?"

"Is it possible," said the Ass, shaking its ears, "that you don't know how it has succeeded in making itself liked, and in becoming distinguished? Why, I have guessed the reason. If it hadn't been distinguished for its long ears, it never would have got into favour."

THE WOLF AND THE MOUSE.

A GRISLY Wolf carried off a sheep from the fold into
a retired nook in the forest—not from hospitality,
one may well suppose. The glutton tore the skin off the
poor sheep, and began devouring it so greedily that the
bones cracked under its teeth. But, in spite of its rapacity,
it could not eat it all up; so it set aside what remained over
for supper, and then, lying down close by it, cuddled itself
together at its ease, after the succulent repast.

But, see, the smell of the banquet has attracted its near
neighbour, a young Mouse. Between the mossy tufts and hillocks it has crept, has seized a morsel of meat, and has run

off quickly to its home in a hollow tree.   Perceiving the theft, our Wolf begins to howl through the forest, crying, "Police!   Robbery!   Stop thief!   I'm ruined!   I've been robbed of everything I possessed!"

Just such an occurrence did I witness in the town.   A thief stole a watch from Clement, the judge, and the judge shouted after the thief, "Police, police!"

THE PEASANT IN TROUBLE

A THIEF crept into a Peasant's house one autumn night, and, betaking himself to the store-room,* rummaged the walls, the shelves, and the ceiling, and stole, without remorse, all he could lay his hands on. So that our Moujik, poor fellow, who had lain down a rich man, woke up so bereft of everything, that a beggar's sack seemed the only resource left him in the world. Heaven grant that none of us may ever know a similar waking! The Peasant weeps and wails, and calls together his friends and relatives, his gossips, and all his neighbours.

"Can't you help me in my trouble?" he asks.

Then each begins to address the Peasant, and favours him with sage advice.

Says his gossip Karpich, "Ah, my light! you shouldn't have gone boasting to all the world that you were so rich."

Says his gossip Klimich, "In future, my dear gossip, you must take care to have the store-room close to the room you sleep in."

———————————

* The *Klict* is a sort of general store-room, serving the purposes of a larder a clothes-press, &c.

"Ah, brothers, you're all in the wrong," exclaims his neighbour Phocas. "The fault wasn't in the store-room being at a distance. What you must do is to keep some fierce dogs in your yard. Take whichever you please of my Jouchka's puppies. I would far rather cordially make a present of them to a good neighbour than drown them."

And thus, as far as words went, his loving friends and relatives gave him a thousand excellent pieces of advice, each according to his power; but when it came to deeds, not one of them would help the poor fellow.

THE SWORD-BLADE.

THE keen blade of a Sword, made of Damascus steel, which had been thrown aside on a heap of old iron, was sent to market with the other pieces of metal, and sold for a trifle to a Moujik. Now, a Moujik's ideas move in a narrow circle. He immediately set to work to turn the blade, to account. Our Moujik fitted a handle to the blade, and began to strip with it lime trees, in the forest, of the bark he wanted for shoes, while at home he unceremoniously splintered fir chips with it. Sometimes, also, he would lop off twigs with it, or small branches for mending his wattled fences, or would shape stakes with it for his garden paling.

And the result was that, before the year was out, our blade was notched and rusted from one end to the other, and the children used to ride astride of it.   So one day a Hedgehog, which was lying under a bench in the cottage, close by the spot where the blade had been flung, said to it,

"Tell me, what do you think of this life of yours? If there is any truth in all the fine things that are said about Damascus steel, you surely must be ashamed of having to splinter fir chips, and square stakes, and of being turned, at last, into a plaything for children."

But the Sword-blade replied,

" In the hands of a warrior, I should have been a terror to the foe ; but here my special faculties are of no avail.   So in this house I am turned to base uses only.   But am I free to choose my employment ?   No !   Not I, but he, ought to be ashamed, who could not see for what I was fit to be employed."

THE RAIN-CLOUD.

A GREAT Cloud passed rapidly over a country which was parched by heat, but did not let fall a single drop to refresh it. Presently it poured a copious stream of rain into the sea, and then began boasting of its generosity in the hearing of a neighbouring Mountain. But the Mountain replied,

"What good have you done by such generosity? and now can one help being pained at seeing it? If you had poured your showers over the land, you would have saved a whole district from famine. But as to the sea, my friend, it has plenty of water already, without you adding to it."

[This fable is said to have been written on the occasion of certain grants of land made to the Governor of the Province of Pskof, during the prevalence of a terrible famine in that part of the country.]

THE WHISK.

GREAT honours were suddenly conferred upon a dirty Whisk.* It will not now any longer sweep the floors of kitchens; for the master's caftans are handed over to it, the servants having, probably, got drunk. Well, our Whisk set to work vigorously. It was never tired of belabouring the master's clothes, and it thrashed the caftans like so much rye. Undoubtedly its industry was great; only the misfortune was, that it was itself so dirty. Of what use, then, was all its toil? The more it tried to clean anything, the dirtier did it make it.

Just as much harm is done when a fool interferes in what is out of his own line, and undertakes to correct the work of a man of learning.

---

* In Russian, a *Golik*. This is a provincial word, a native of the Province of Smolensk. The *Golik* is a bunch of bare twigs—*goly* meaning bare—greatly resembling our scholastic birch. The Russians make great use of it in their baths (see Dal's " Explanatory Lexicon of the living Great Russian Language," a work of the greatest value to every one who wishes to become really well acquainted with Russian literature.)

THE EAGLE AND THE SPIDER.

AN EAGLE had soared above the clouds to the loftiest
peak of the Caucasus. There, on an ancient cedar
it settled, and admired the landscape visible at its feet. It
seemed as if the borders of the world could be seen from
thence. Here flowed rivers, winding across the plains; there
stood woods and meadows, adorned with the full garb of
spring; and, beyond, frowned the angry Caspian Sea, black
as a raven's wing.

"Praise be to thee, O Jove, that, as ruler of the world,
thou hast bestowed on me such powers of flight that I know
of no heights to me inaccessible!"—thus the Eagle addressed

Jupiter—"insomuch that I now look upon the beauties of the world from a point whither no other being has ever flown."

"What a boaster you are!" replies a Spider to it from a twig. "As I sit here, am I lower than you, comrade?"

The Eagle looks up. Truly enough, the Spider is busy spinning its web about a twig overhead, just as if it wanted to shut out the sunlight from the Eagle.

"How did you get up to this height?" asks the Eagle. "Even among the strongest of wing there are some who would not dare to trust themselves here. But you, weak and wingless, is it possible you can have crawled here?"

"No; I didn't use that means of rising aloft."

"Well, then, how did you get here?"

"Why, I just fastened myself on to you, and you brought me yourself from down below on your tail-feathers. But I know how to maintain my position here without your help, so I beg you will not assume such airs in my presence; for know that I——"

At this moment a gust of wind comes suddenly flying by, and whirls away the Spider again into the lowest depths.

THE MERCHANT.

"COME here, Andrew, my brother! Where have you got to? Come here, quickly, and admire your uncle's doings. Deal as I do, and you'll never suffer loss." Thus in his shop spoke a Merchant to his nephew. "You know that remnant of Polish cloth—the one we have had on our hands so long, because it was old, and damp, and rotten? Well, I've just passed it off for English. Here is a hundred-rouble note I have just this instant got for it. Heaven must have sent a fool this way."

"Just so, uncle, just so," replied the nephew; "only I'm

not quite sure as to which was the fool.　Just look here; you 'll see you 've taken a forged note."

To cheat!—the Merchant cheated : there 's nothing wonderful in that.　But if one looks around in the world a little higher than where the shops are, one sees that even there people go on in the self-same manner.　Almost all of them are occupied in everything by the same calculation ; and that is, " How can one man best succeed in cheating another?"

THE PIG.

A PIG once made its way into the courtyard of a lordly mansion, sauntered at its will around the stables and the kitchen, wallowed in filth, bathed in slops, and then returned home from its visit a thorough pig.

"Well, Kavronya, what have you seen?" says the Swineherd to the Pig. "They do say that there is nothing but pearls and diamonds* in rich people's houses, and that there each thing is richer than the rest."

---

* One of Krilof's Russian critics, who has attacked this fable as being "low," finds

" I assure you they talk nonsense," grunted Kavronya. " I
saw no riches at all—nothing but dirt and offal ; and yet
you may suppose I didn't spare my snout, for I dug up the
whole of the back yard."

God forbid I should hurt any one by my comparison ; but
how can one help calling those critics Kavronyas who, in
whatever they have to discuss, have the faculty of seeing
only that which is bad?

.

fault with the two words *biser* and *jemchug*, used here by the Swineherd to describe
something precious, saying that they both mean pearls.   His remark holds good for
the old Slavonic ; but in modern Russian *biser* means glass beads of various colours
used for stringing, and *jemchug*, the real pearl.

THE FOX IN THE ICE.

VERY early one winter morning, during a hard frost, a Fox was drinking at an ice-hole, not far from the haunts of men. Meanwhile, whether by pure accident or from negligence doesn't much matter, the end of its tail got wet, and froze to the ice. No great harm was done; the Fox could easily remedy it. It had only to give a tolerably hard pull, and leave about a score of its hairs behind; then it could run away home quickly, before any one came. But how could it make up its mind to spoil its tail? Such a bushy tail as it was, so ample and golden! No; better wait a little. Surely, men are sleeping still. It's even possible that a thaw may, meanwhile, set in. In that case, it will be able to withdraw its tail easily from the ice-hole. So it waits: it goes on waiting, but its tail only freezes all the more. It looks round; the day is already beginning to dawn. People are stirring; voices are to be heard. Our poor Fox begins to rush about wildly—now this way, now that. But still it cannot free itself from the hole. Luckily, a Wolf comes running that way.

"Dear friend, gossip, father!" cries the Fox, "do save me I am all but lost!"

8

So the Wolf stopped, and set to work to rescue the Fox. Its method was a very simple one : it bit the tail of the Fox clean off. So our foolish friend went home tailless, but rejoicing that its skin was still on its back.

MIRON.

THERE lived in a certain city a rich man, named Miron. Against this rich man arose complaints from his neighbours on all sides. And the neighbours were so far right that, although he had millions in his strong box, he never gave a copeck to the poor.

But who is there who does not like to gain a good reputation? In order to give a different turn to the conversation about him, our Miron made it publicly known among the people, that in future he meant to give away food to the needy every Saturday. And, indeed, any one who passed his house, at the end of the week, could see that his gates were not closed.

"Poor fellow!" they think, "he will be utterly ruined." But of that there was no fear; for, every Saturday, he unchained a number of ferocious dogs, so that it was not a question with the poor who visited him of eating or of drinking, but simply of escaping, if Heaven willed it, with a whole skin.

In the meantime, Miron was looked upon as almost a saint. Every one said, "One can't sufficiently admire Miron; only it's a pity that he keeps such savage dogs, and that it's so difficult to get at him : otherwise, he is ready to give away all he has, even to the uttermost copeck."

It has often occurred to me to see how hard of access are the palaces of great people. But, of course, the fault is not due to the Mirons. It is always the dogs who are to blame.

THE WOLF AND THE FOX.

A FOX, which had feasted on fowls to satiety, and had set aside a good store of spare food, lay down under a haycock, one evening, to sleep. Suddenly it looks up, and sees a hungry Wolf dragging itself along to pay it a visit.

"This is terrible, gossip!" says the Wolf. "I cannot anywhere find even the smallest of bones to pick, and I am actually dying of hunger. The dogs are malicious, the shepherd won't sleep, and I have nothing left but to hang myself."

"Really?"

"Really and truly."

"My poor old gossip! But won't you take a little hay?

There is a whole haycock. I am delighted to oblige my friend."

But what its friend wanted was meat, not hay; and about its stock of provisions the Fox said never a word. So my grey-coated hero, though greatly caressed as to its ears by its gossip, had to go to bed supperless.

THE OWL AND THE ASS.

A BLIND Ass, which had undertaken a long journey, wandered from the road into a forest. As the night came on, our foolish fellow went so far into the thicket that it couldn't move either backwards or forwards; and even one who had eyes would have been unable to get out of that difficulty. But an Owl, by good luck, happened to be in the neighbourhood, and offered to act as a guide to the Ass. We all know how well Owls see at night. Hills, hillocks, ditches, precipices—all these our Owl distinguished as if it had been daylight, and, by daybreak, it had made its way with the Ass to the level road. Now, how could any one part with such a guide? So the Ass entreated the Owl not to desert it, ar d determined to visit the whole world in the Owl's company. Our Owl seated itself like a lord on the back of the Ass, and the two friends began to continue their journey. But did it prosper? No. The sun had scarcely begun to glow in the morning sky, when a greater than nocturnal darkness hid everything from the Owl's eyes. But our Owl is obstinate : it directs the Ass at random.

"Take care !" it cries. "We shall tumble into a pool, if we go to the right."

There was really no pool on the right ; but on the left there was even worse.

"Keep more to the left—another pace to the left!"

And--the Owl and the Ass fell into the ravine together.

THE MONKEY AND THE SPECTACLES.

A MONKEY became weak-sighted in old age. Now it had heard men say that this misfortune was one of no great importance; only one must provide oneself with glasses. So it gets half-a-dozen pairs of spectacles, turns them now this way and now that, puts them on the top of its head, applies them to its tail, smells them, licks them; still the spectacles have no effect at all on its sight.

"Good lack!" it cries, "what fools they be who listen to all the nonsense men utter! They've told me nothing but lies about the spectacles. There isn't an atom of good in them."

Here the Monkey, in its vexation and annoyance, flung them down on a stone so violently that they were utterly broken to bits.

Unfortunately, men behave in the same way.   However useful a thing may be, an ignorant man, who knows nothing about its value, is sure to speak ill of it, and, if he possesses any influence, he persecutes it too.

THE ELEPHANT AND THE PUG-DOG.

AN Elephant was being taken through the streets, probably as a sight. It is well known that Elephants are a wonder among us; so crowds of gaping idlers followed the Elephant. From some corner or other, a Pug-dog comes to meet him. It looks at the Elephant, and then begins to run at it, to bark, to squeal, to try to get at it, just as if it wanted to fight it.

"Neighbour, cease to bring shame on yourself," says Shafka * to it. "Are you capable of fighting an Elephant? Just see now, you are already hoarse; but it keeps straight on, and does not pay you the slightest attention."

"Aye, aye!" replies the Pug-dog, "that's just what gives me courage. In this way, you see, without fighting at all, I may get reckoned among the greatest bullies. Just let the dogs say, 'Ah, look at Puggy! He must be strong, indeed, that's clear, or he would never bark at an Elephant.'"

* Name given to a long-haired dog.

THE INDUSTRIOUS BEAR.

SEEING that a Peasant, who employed himself in making dugas,* disposed of them advantageously, a Bear determined to gain its living by the same business. The forest resounded with knocking and cracking, and the noise of the Bear's pranks could be heard a verst off. It destroyed a prodigious number of elms, birches, and hazels; but its labours did not lead to a good result. (For dugas are bent by dint of patience, and not in a moment.) So our Bear goes to the Peasant, and asks his advice, saying,

"Neighbour, what is the reason of this? I can break trees; but I haven't been able to bend one into a duga. Tell me, in what does the real secret of success consist?"

"In that," answered the Peasant, "of which, my friend, you haven't a bit—in patience."

---

* The *duga* is the wooden arch which, in a Russian cart or carriage, rises from the shafts above the horse's neck. When gaily painted and provided with bells, it is supposed to appeal to the animal's æsthetic tastes, and to encourage it to go on its way rejoicing. There are factories now in which *dugas* are made wholesale by steam-power.

THE FOX AS ARCHITECT.

A CERTAIN Lion was exceedingly fond of fowls, but they never throve with him. And that was no wonder. They lived utterly free from all restrictions; and so some of them were stolen, others disappeared of their own accord.

To remedy this unpleasantness and loss, the Lion determined to build a large poultry-yard, and so cunningly to design and arrange it, as entirely to keep out thieves, but to provide the fowls with plenty of space and all things needful.

Well, they inform the Lion that the Fox is a great hand at building, so the affair is entrusted to him. The building is begun and ended successfully, the Fox working at it with all conceivable industry and talent. The building is looked at and examined in detail. Truly, it is a work which cannot be too much admired. Everything is there which any one can possibly desire — food close at hand, perches inserted everywhere, refuges from cold and heat, and retired little places for the sitting hens. All honour and glory to our good Fox ! A liberal reward is bestowed on him, and an order is given to transfer the fowls, without loss of time, to their new abode.

But is the change of any use? Not at all. It is true that

the building seems firm and massive, and the walls enclosing it lofty. But yet the fowls daily become fewer and fewer. No one can imagine whence this evil springs. But the Lion orders a watch to be set; and whom do they catch? Why that villain, the Fox. It is true that he had constructed the building so that no one else could break in and steal; but he had taken care to leave a little hole by which he could get into it himself.

FORTUNE'S VISIT.

A T the extremity of a town stood a wretched old house. In it lived three brothers, who could not get rich. Somehow, there was not a single thing that succeeded with them. Whatever any one of them took in hand was sure to prove unsuccessful : on all sides they met with hindrance and loss; and, according to them, it was all the fault of Fortune.

It happened that Fortune paid them a visit as she was passing by, and, touched by their great poverty, determined to do all she could to help them in everything they under-took, and to spend a whole summer with them. A whole

summer!—a long time indeed. Well, the poor fellows soon
find their affairs assuming a different aspect. One of them,
although he was a poor hand at trading, gets a great profit
now on everything he either buys or sells, utterly forgets that
such a thing as loss exists, and rapidly becomes as rich as
Crœsus. The second enters the public service. At another
time he would have stuck fast among the copyists; but now
he reaps successes on all sides. Every time he gives a
dinner, or pays a visit of ceremony, he gets either rank conferred upon him or a place given him. See, he has an
estate, a mansion in town, and a box in the country

And now you will ask, what advantage did the third
brother obtain? I suppose that Fortune really helped him
also? Certainly; from his side she scarcely ever absented
herself. The third brother chased flies all the summer, and
that with the most wonderful success. I don't know whether
he used to be clever at that sort of thing in former days, but
during that summer his labour was never thrown away. In
whatever manner he moved his hand (thanks to Fortune), he
never once missed his shot.

But see! their guest, meanwhile, has brought her stay
with the brothers to an end, and has set out on a long
journey. Two of the brothers have gained greatly. One
of them is rich; the other has got riches and rank besides.
But the third brother curses his fate, inasmuch as malignant
Fortune has left him nothing but a beggar's wallet.

THE LION, THE CHAMOIS, AND THE FOX.

A LION was chasing a Chamois along a valley. He
had all but caught it, and with longing eyes was
anticipating a certain and a satisfying repast. It seemed as
if it were utterly impossible for the victim to escape; for a
deep ravine appeared to bar the way for both the hunter and
the hunted. But the nimble Chamois, gathering together all
its strength, shot like an arrow from a bow across the
chasm, and stood still on the rocky cliff on the other side.
Our Lion pulled up short. But at that moment a friend of
his happened to be near at hand. That friend was the Fox.

"What!" said he, "with your strength and agility, is it

9

possible that you will yield to a feeble Chamois? You have only to will, and you will be able to work wonders. Though the abyss be deep, yet, if you are only in earnest, I am certain you will clear it. Surely you can confide in my disinterested friendship. I would not expose your life to danger if I were not so well aware of your strength and dexterity."

The Lion's blood waxed hot, and began to boil in his veins. He flung himself with all his might into space. But he could not clear the chasm; so down he tumbled headlong, and was killed by the fall. Then what did his dear friend do? He cautiously made his way down to the bottom of the ravine, and there, out in the open space and the free air, seeing that the Lion wanted neither flattery nor obedience now, he set to work to pay the last sad rites to his dead friend, and in a month picked his bones clean.

THE ORACLE.

IN a certain temple there was a wooden idol which began to utter prophetic answers, and to give wise counsels. Accordingly, it rejoiced in a very rich attire, being covered from top to toe with gold and silver; and was gorged with sacrifices, deafened by prayers, and choked with incense. Every one believed blindly in the Oracle.

All of a sudden—wonderful to relate!—the Oracle began to talk nonsense—took to answering incoherently and absurdly, so that, if any one consulted it about anything, whatever our Oracle said was a lie; so that every one wondered what had become of its prophetic faculty. The fact was, that the idol was hollow, and the priests used to sit in it in order to reply to the laity; and so, as long as the priest was discreet, the idol did not talk nonsense; but when a fool took to sitting in it, the idol became a mere dummy.*

I have heard—can it be true?—that in days gone by there used to be judges who were renowned for ability—so long as they kept an able secretary.

---

* The word used is *bolvan*—the term irreverently applied by the common folk in Russia to most of their outdoor statues.

THE ASS AND THE PEASANT.

A PEASANT, who had hired an Ass for his garden during the summer, set it to drive away the impudent race of crows and of sparrows. The Ass was one of a most honest character, utterly unacquainted with either rapacity or theft. It never profited by a single leaf belonging to its master, and it would indeed be a sin to say that it connived at the proceedings of the birds. Still the Peasant got but little good out of his garden. The Ass, as it chased the birds with all its might, galloped across all the beds, backwards and forwards, in such a manner that it trod underfoot and trampled in pieces everything that grew in the garden.

Seeing then that all his pains were thrown away, the Peasant took a cudgel and revenged himself for his loss on the back of the Ass. "No wonder!" says every one; "serve the beast right! Was it for a creature of its parts to undertake such a business?"

But I say—though not with the intention of defending the Ass; it was certainly in fault, and it has already paid the penalty—surely he also was to blame who set the Ass to guard his garden.

THE SHEEP AND THE DOGS.

IN a certain flock of Sheep, it was resolved that the number of dogs should be increased, in order that the wolves might worry no more. What was the result? Why, the number increased so greatly that at last, truly enough, the Sheep were no longer annoyed by the wolves. But dogs, too, must live. So, first, they deprived the Sheep of their fleeces, and then they tore their skins off them, choosing them by lot. At last, only five or six of the Sheep remained, and those also the dogs ate up.

[In former days, whenever there was a difficulty about setting straight anything that had gone wrong in Russia, the only idea which suggested itself to the minds of the authorities was to increase the number of those officials who had to deal with the matter. But as these officials were miserably paid, they had to make a livelihood out of the people who were confided to their charge, and who, accordingly, fared no better than the sheep in the fable. Latterly, a different system has been introduced, and fewer but better paid officials are now employed.]

THE STRING OF CARTS.

A NUMBER of Carts, laden with pottery, were going along in a string, and had to descend a steep hill. Having left the others to wait a little on the top of the hill, the owner began very cautiously to lead down the first cart. The good horse which drew it almost supported the weight on its croup, not allowing it to roll down too fast. But a young Horse up on top took to blaming the poor animal for every step it made :

"Ah, praiseworthy animal! how wonderful! Just see, it crawls like a crab. See there, it has almost stumbled over a stone! Look how awry, how askew, are its movements!

Ah! it's bolder now. There's a jostle again! Only here you ought to have gone a little more to the left. Oh, what a donkey! It would be all very well if this were night, or if it were going uphill. But now it is going downhill, and by daylight. One loses all patience while watching it. Really it's a water-carrier you ought to be, if you have no sense in you. But just look at us!—see how we will dash along. Never fear for us; we wont lose a moment: we shall not so much carry our loads as whirl them down."

With these words, straining its back and inflating its chest, the young Horse sets its load in motion. But no sooner does it commence the descent than the weight begins to press upon it heavily, the Cart to roll rapidly. The Horse, urged on from behind, and thrust from side to side, dashes on splendidly at a gallop. Over stones, across gullies, went the Cart amid shocks and boundings. More to the left—still to the left, till at last the Cart and its load goes headlong into the ditch with a crash! Farewell to the master's crockery.

[This fable alludes to the criticisms evoked by Kutuzof's unwillingness to precipitate matters in dealing with Napoleon. When he refused to fight under the walls of Moscow, the people began to clamour against him, as they had done against Barclay de Tolly; and the younger officers under his command were especially indignant with him. But Krilof took his part throughout.]

THE DIVERS.

A CERTAIN King, says Krilof,* could not make up his mind as to whether knowledge and science produce more good or harm. He consulted divers learned men on the subject, but they could not solve the problem to his satisfaction. At last, one day, he met a venerable and remarkably intelligent hermit, to whom he confided his doubts, and who favoured him with the following apologue:

"There was once a fisherman, in India, who lived on the sea-coast. After a long life of poverty and privation, he died, leaving three sons. They, seeing that their nets brought them in but a scanty livelihood, and detesting their father's avocation, determined to make the sea yield them a richer recompense—not fish, but pearls. So, as they knew how to swim and to dive, they gave themselves up to collecting that form of tribute from it. But the three brothers met with very different kinds of success.

"The first, the laziest of the family, spent his time in sauntering along the shore. He had an objection to wetting even so much as his feet, so he confined his expectations to picking

---

* I have thought it best to abridge the introduction, which is of inordinate length in the original.

up such pearls as the waves might wash ashore at his feet.
But the result of this laziness of his was that he scarcely made
enough to keep him alive. As to the second, he used to
dive, and find rich pearls at the bottom of the sea, never
sparing any pains, and knowing how to choose those depths
only which it lay within his power to sound.

"But the third brother, troubled by a craving after vast
treasures, reasoned with himself as follows : 'It is true that
there are pearls which one can find near the shore ; but what
treasures, apparently, might I not expect if I could only succeed in reaching the lowest depths of the open sea ! There,
no doubt, lie heaps of countless riches—corals, pearls, and
precious stones—all of which one might pick up and carry
away at will.' Captivated by this idea, the foolish fellow
straightway sought the open sea, chose the spot where the
depths seemed blackest, and plunged into the abyss. But
his recklessness cost him his life ; for the deep swallowed him
down, and he never returned to the light of day.

"O King," continued the hermit, "no doubt we recognise
in knowledge the source of many benefits. But those who
seek it in an irreverent spirit may find in it an abyss in
which they may perish, like the diver, but with this difference, that they may too often involve others in their own
ruin."

THE TRIGAMIST.

A CERTAIN sinner, while his wife was still alive, married two other women. As soon as the news of this reached the King, who was a severe king, and disinclined to permit such scandals, he immediately ordered the polygamist to be tried for the offence, and ordained that such a punishment should be discovered for him as would terrify the whole people, so that no one should in future be capable of attempting so great a crime. "But if I see that his punishment is a light one," he added, "then I will hang all the judges around the judgment-seat."

This pleasantry is disagreeable to the judges. Fear bathes

them in a cold sweat.   For three whole days they deliberate
as to what punishment can be contrived for the culprit.   Pun-
ishments are plentiful ; but experience has proved that none
of them will deter people from sinning.   However, at last
Heaven inspired them.   The criminal was brought into court
for the announcement of the judicial decision, by which they
unanimously decreed—

That he should live with all his three wives at once !

At such a decision the people were lost in astonishment,
and expected that the King would hang all the judges.   But,
before the fifth day arrived, the Trigamist had hanged himself.   And the sentence produced such alarm that since that
time no man has committed trigamy in that country.

[This fable is not altogether original, being founded on a
misogynical pleasantry of great antiquity; but it is given as
a specimen of Krilof's terse style of story-telling.]

THE CUCKOO AND THE TURTLE-DOVE.

A CUCKOO sat on a bough, bitterly complaining. "Why art thou so sad, dear friend?" sympathisingly cooed the Turtle-dove to her, from a neighbouring twig. "Is it because spring has passed away from us, and love with it; that the sun has sunk lower, and that we are nearer to the winter?"

"How can I help grieving, unhappy one that I am?" replies the Cuckoo: "thou shalt thyself be the judge. This spring my love was a happy one, and, after a while, I became a mother. But my offspring utterly refuse even to recognise me. Was it such a return that I expected from them? And how can I help being envious when I see how ducklings crowd around their mother—how chickens hasten to the hen when she calls to them. Just like an orphan I sit here, utterly alone, and know not what filial affection means."

"Poor thing!" says the Dove, "I pity you from my heart. As for me, though I know such things often occur, I should die outright if my dovelets did not love me. But tell me, have you already brought up your little ones? When did you find time to build a nest? I never saw you doing anything of the kind: you were always flying and fluttering about."

"Yes, indeed!" says the Cuckoo. "Pretty nonsense it would have been if I had spent such fine days in sitting on a nest! That would, indeed, have been the highest pitch of stupidity! I always laid my eggs in the nests of other birds."

"Then how can you expect your little ones to care for you?" says the Turtle-dove.

Fathers and mothers! let this fable read you a lesson. I have not written it as an excuse for undutiful children. Irreverence on their part, and want of love towards their parents, must always be a great fault. But, if they have grown up apart from you, and you have entrusted their education to hireling hands, have not you yourselves to blame, if in old age you obtain but little happiness from them?

THE LEAVES AND THE ROOTS.

ON a beautiful summer day, the Leaves on a tree whispered softly to the zephyrs; and, as their shadow fell upon the valley, thus did they speak, vaunting their luxuriant verdure:

"Is it not true that we are the pride of the whole valley? Is it not by us that this tree is rendered so bushy and wide-spreading, so stately and majestic? What would it be without us? Yes, indeed; we may praise ourselves without committing a sin! Do not we, by our cool shade, protect the shepherd and the traveller from the heat? Do not we, by our beauty, attract the shepherdess to dance here? From among us, in the morning and the evening twilight, the nightingale sings; and as to you, zephyrs, you scarcely ever desert us."

"You might add a word of thanks even to us," answered a feeble voice from underground.

"Who is it that dares thus audaciously to call us to account? Who are you who are talking there?" the Leaves began to lisp, noisily tossing on the tree.

"We are they," was the reply from down below, "who, burrowing in darkness here, provide you with nourishment.

Is it possible that you do not recognise us? We are the roots of the tree on which you flourish. Go on rejoicing in your beauty : only remember there is this difference between us, that with the new spring a new foliage is born ; but, if the roots perish, neither you nor the tree can survive."

[In the large illustrated edition of the fables, published four years ago, at St. Petersburg, this story is accompanied by one of Trutofsky's spirited drawings, which renders its meaning very clear. A couple of gentlemen and a lady, evidently belonging to the proprietor class, are sitting at their ease in a balcony ; and down below, regarded by them with contemptuous wonder, stand half-a-dozen peasants, their clothes tattered, their figures emaciated, their faces worn with care. The fable was written in 1811, at a time when the question of the emancipation of the serfs was occupying considerable attention.]

THE WOLF AND THE CUCKOO.

"FAREWELL, neighbour!" said a Wolf to a Cuckoo. "In vain have I deluded myself with the idea of finding peace in this spot. Your people and dogs are all alike here—one worse than the other: even if you were an angel, you couldn't help quarrelling with them."

"And is my neighbour going far? and where is that people so pious that you think you will be able to live in harmony with them?"

"Oh! I am going right away to the forest of the happy Arcadia. There, it is said, they don't know what war is. The men are as mild as lambs, and the rivers flow with no-

10

thing but milk. There, in a word, the Age of Gold is to be found. Every one treats his neighbour like a brother; and it is even said that the dogs never bark there, much less bite. Tell me, dear friend, would it not be charming to find one-self, even in a dream, in so peaceful a land as that? Fare-well! Don't retain an unpleasant remembrance of me. There I shall really be able to live in harmony, in plenty, and in indulgence, and not, as here, have to be always on guard by day, and be deprived of one's quiet repose at night."

"A happy journey to you, dear neighbour," says the Cuckoo. "But, tell me, do you leave your teeth and your habits behind you, or do you take them with you?"

"How could I possibly leave them behind me? What nonsense are you talking?"

"Then, mark my words! your skin won't remain long on your back there."

THE IMPIOUS.

IN the days of old there was a people, to the shame, be it said, of the nations of the earth, which became so hardened in heart, that it took up arms against the gods. Noisily, with countless banners displayed, the insurgent crowds overrun the plains, some armed with bows, others with slings. In order to kindle more fury among the people, the ringleaders, in the insolence of their hearts, declare that the tribunal of Heaven is harsh and foolish—that the gods either sleep or judge unreasonably—that the time has come to read them an unceremonious lesson—and that, as to the rest, it will not be difficult to hurl stones at the gods from the nearest hills, and to fill all Olympus with arrows.

Disquieted by the insolent blasphemies these fools uttered, all Olympus applied to Jupiter with the prayer that he would avert this evil. And even all the heavenly council was of opinion that, in order to confute the rebels, it would not be amiss to make manifest, at all events, a little miracle—a deluge or an earthquake, with thunder and lightning, or, perhaps, to crush them under a shower of stones.

"Let us wait a little," replied Jupiter; "for if they do not become quiet, but go on with their foolish violence, not fearing the immortals, they will be punished by their own deeds."

1 —2

Then, with a roar, the banded rebels against the gods shot into the air a mass of arrows, a cloud of stones. But, laden with innumerable deaths, inevitable and terrible, their weapons fell back again upon their own heads.

THE FOX AND THE MARMOT.

"WHERE are you running so fast, gossip, without ever looking back?" a Marmot asked a Fox.

"Oh, my friend, my dear gossip, I have had a calumnious accusation brought against me, and I have been dismissed as an extortioner. You know, I was the judge of the poultry-yard. In that position I lost my health and my peace of mind. From the press of business, I never had time to get a comfortable meal, and at nights I could not sleep soundly. And now, in return for this, I have incurred the wrath of my employers, and all on account of a calumny. Only just think! Who in the world shall be without reproach, if calumnies are listened to? I an extortioner! Do they suppose I've gone out of my mind? Now, I appeal to you, have you ever seen that I took part in that wickedness? Think the matter over; reflect on it well."

"No, gossip, no; but I have often remarked that there was some down on your muzzle."

Many an official complains that he is forced to spend every rouble he has; and all the town knows that, originally, he had nothing, and that he got nothing with his wife. But see ! little by little he builds a house ; he buys an estate. Now, in what manner can you reconcile his salary with his expenditure ?   Although you can prove nothing against him legally, yet you will not be committing a sin if you say, "That fellow has down on his muzzle."

THE PEASANT AND THE ROBBER.

A PEASANT, who was beginning to stock his little farm,
had bought a cow and a milk-pail at a fair, and was
going quietly homewards by a lonely path through the forest,
when he suddenly fell into the hands of a Robber. The
Robber stripped him as bare as a lime tree.*

"Have mercy!" cried the Peasant. "I am utterly ruined.
You have reduced me to beggary. For a whole year I have

* *i.e.*, Bare as a lime tree after it has been stripped of its bark, of which the peasants
make shoes, baskets, &c.

worked to buy this dear little cow.   I could scarcely bear to
wait for this day to arrive."

"Very good," replied the Robber, touched by compassion;
"don't cry out against me. After all, I shall not want to milk
your cow, so I 'll give you back your milk-pail."

THE ANT.

A CERTAIN Ant had extraordinary strength, such as had never been heard of even in the days of old. It could even, as its trustworthy historian states, lift up two large grains of barley at once! Besides this, it was also remarkable for wonderful courage. Whenever it saw a worm, it immediately stuck its claws into it, and it would even go alone against a spider. And so it acquired such a reputation on its ant-hill, that it became the sole subject of conversation.

Extravagant praise I consider poison; but our ant was not of the same opinion: it delighted in it, measured it by its own conceit, and believed the whole of it. At length its head became so turned that it determined to exhibit itself to the neighbouring city, that it might acquire fame by showing off its strength there.

Perched on the top of a lofty cart-load of hay, having proudly made its way to the side of the moujik in charge, it enters the city in great state. But, alas! what a blow to its pride! It had imagined that the whole bazaar would run together to see it, as to a fire. But not a word is said about it, every one being absorbed in his own business. Our Ant seizes a leaf, and jerks it about, tumbles down, leaps up

again. Still not a soul pays it any attention. At last, wearied
with exerting itself, and holding itself proudly erect, it says,
with vexation, to Barbos, the mastiff, lying beside its master's
cart, "It must be confessed, mustn't it, that the people of
your city have neither eyes nor brains? Can it really be true
that no one remarks me, although I have been straining myself here for a whole hour? And yet I'm sure that at home
I am well known to the whole of the ant-hill."

And so it went back again, utterly crestfallen.

THE SLANDERER AND THE SNAKE.

ON the occasion of some triumphal procession in the realms below, the Snake and the Slanderer refused to yield each other precedence, and began a noisy quarrel as to which of the two had the best right to go first.

Now, in the infernal regions, as is well known, he takes precedence who has done most harm to his fellow-creatures. So in this hot and serious dispute, the Slanderer showed his tongue to the Snake; and the Snake boastingly talked to the Slanderer about its sting, hissed out that it was unable to put up with an affront, and strove hard to crawl past him. The Slanderer actually found himself being left behind. But Beelzebub could not allow this: he himself took the Slanderer's part, and drove the Snake back, saying,

"Although I recognise your merit, yet I justly assign precedence to him. You are excessively venomous, and dangerous in the extreme to everything which is near you; your sting is fatal, and you sting—which is no small merit—without provocation. But can you wound from afar, like the deadly tongue of the Slanderer, from whom there is no escape, even though mountains or oceans intervene? It is clear, then, that he is more deadly than you; so give place to him, and in future behave more quietly."

Since that time, Slanderers have been honoured more than Snakes in hell.

[In the first edition of this fable, which appeared in May, 1814, the triumphal procession was represented as taking place " on the birthday of Attila or Nero, or perhaps of Napoleon : I am afraid of stating which, for fear of making a mistake. But, after all, it 's no matter. In Satan's realms, such names are inscribed on a tablet, and great solemnities are appointed in their honour."

Krilof was "a good hater;" and he certainly did not like Napoleon.]

THE TWO DOGS

BARBOS, the faithful yard-dog, who serves his master zealously, happens to see his old acquaintance Joujou, the curly lap-dog, seated at the window on a soft down cushion. Sidling fondly up to her, like a child to a parent, he all but weeps with emotion; and there, under the window, he whines, wags his tail, and bounds about.

"What sort of a life do you lead now, Joujoutka, ever since the master took you into his mansion? You remember, no doubt, we used often to suffer hunger out in the yard. What is your present service like?"

" It would be a sin in me to murmur against my good fortune," answers Joujoutka. "My master cannot make enough of me. I live amidst riches and plenty, and I eat and drink off silver. I frolic with the master, and, if I get tired, I take my ease on carpets or on a soft couch. And how do you get on?"

"I?" replied Barbos, letting his tail dangle like a whip, and hanging his head. "I live as I used to do. I suffer from cold and hunger; and here, while guarding my master's house, I have to sleep at the foot of the wall, and I get drenched in the rain. And if I bark at the wrong time, I am whipped. But how did you, Joujou, who were so small and weak, get taken into favour, while I jump out of my skin to no purpose? What is it you do?"

"'What is it you do?' A pretty question to ask!" replied Joujou, mockingly. "I walk upon my hind legs."

[This fable is suspiciously like that by Izmailof, called "The Two Cats," which, in its turn, was adapted from Florian.]

THE STONE AND THE WORM.

"WHAT a fuss every one is making! How wanting in manners!" observed, with respect to a shower, a Stone which lay in a field. "Have the kindness to look. Every one is delighted with it. They have longed for it as if it were the best of guests; but what is it that it has done? It has come for a couple of hours or so—no more. But they should make a few inquiries about me. Why I have lain here for centuries. Modest and unassuming, I lie quietly where I am thrown. And yet I have never heard from a single person so much as a 'Thank you!' It is not without reason that the world gets reviled. I cannot see a grain of justice anywhere in it."

"Hold your tongue!" exclaimed a Worm. "This shower, brief as it has been, has abundantly watered the fields, which were being rendered sterile by the drought, and has revived the hopes of the farmer. But you contribute nothing to the ground but a useless weight."

Thus many a man will boast of having served the state for forty years; but as for being useful, he has never been a bit more so than the Stone.

THE KITE.

A KITE, which had been allowed to soar to the clouds, called out from on high to a Butterfly down below in the valley,

"I can assure you that I can scarcely make you out. Confess now that you feel envious when you watch my so lofty flight."

"Envious? No, indeed! You have no business to think so much of yourself. You fly high, it is true; but you are always tied by a string. Such a life, my friend, is very far removed from happiness. But I, though in truth but little exalted, fly wherever I wish. I should not like all my life long to have to conduce to some one else's foolish amusement."

THE SQUIRREL IN SERVICE.

A SQUIRREL once served a Lion : I know not how, or
in what capacity. But this much is certain, that the
Squirrel's service found favour in the Lion's eyes ; and to
satisfy the Lion is, certainly, no light affair. In return for
this, it was promised a whole waggon-load of nuts. Promised
—yes ; but, meanwhile, time continues to fly by. Our Squirrel
often suffers hunger, and has tears in its eyes while grinning
in the Lion's presence. When it looks round in the forest,
its former comrades show themselves here and there high up
among the trees. It looks at them till its eyes begin to
blink ; but they keep on always cracking nuts. Our Squirrel

takes a step towards the nut-bushes, looks at them—it can do no more. At one time it is called away, at another it is even dragged off, on the Lion's service.

But see! At last the Squirrel has grown old, and become tedious to the Lion. It is time for it to retire. They have granted the Squirrel its discharge, and they have actually given it the full load of nuts. Excellent nuts—such as the world has never seen before. All picked fruit—one as good as another; a perfect marvel: only one thing is unlucky —the Squirrel has long ago lost all its teeth.

THE PEASANT AND THE AXE.

A MOUJIK, who was building a hut, got vexed with his Axe. The Axe became disagreeable to him; the Moujik waxed wroth. The fact was, he himself hewed abominably; but he lay all the blame on the Axe. Whatever happened, the Moujik found an excuse for scolding it.

"Good-for-nothing creature!" he cries, one day, "from this time forward I will never use you for anything but squaring stakes. Know that, with my cleverness and industry, and my dexterity to boot, I shall get on very well without you, and will cut with a common knife what another wouldn't be able to hew with an axe."

"It is my lot to work at whatever you lay before me," quietly replied the Axe to the angry rebuke, "and so your will, master, is sacred for me. I am ready to serve you in whatever way you please. Only reflect now, that you may not have to repent by-and-bye. You may blunt me on useless labour, if you will; but you will certainly never be able to build huts with a knife."

THE SQUIRREL AND THE THRUSH.

A CROWD collected in a village, one holiday, under the windows of the seignorial mansion, looking, with open-mouthed wonder, at a Squirrel in a revolving cage. A Thrush also was wondering at it, perched on a neighbouring birch tree. The Squirrel ran so fast that his feet seemed to twinkle, and its bushy tail spread itself straight out.

" Dear old compatriot," asked the Thrush, "can you tell me what you are doing there? "

"Oh, dear friend, I have to work hard all day. I am, in fact, the courier of a great noble. So that I can never stop to eat, nor to drink, nor even to take breath;" and the Squirrel betook itself anew to running round in its wheel.

" Yes," said the Thrush, as it flew away, "I can see plainly enough that you are running ; but, for all that, you are always there at the same window."

Look at some busybody or other. He worries himself; he rushes to and fro; every one wonders at him. It seems as if he were going to jump out of his skin ; only, in spite of all that, he does not make any more progress than the Squirrel in the wheel.

THE ASS AND JUPITER.

WHEN Jupiter stocked the universe with the various tribes of animals, the Ass, among others, came into the world. But, either purposely or from an accident owing to the press of work at such a busy time, the Cloud-compeller made a sad mistake, and the Ass came out of its mould no larger than a squirrel. Scarcely any one ever took any notice of the Ass, although the Ass yielded to no one in pride. The Ass was much inclined towards boasting. But what was it to boast of? With such a puny stature, it was ashamed to show itself in the world. So our conceited Ass went to Jupiter, and began to pray for a larger stature.

"Have pity on me!" it cried: "how can I bear this misery? Lions, panthers, elephants, all obtain honour everywhere, and, from the highest to the lowest, every one goes on talking about them only. Why have you treated Asses so unkindly that they never obtain any honour, and not a word is ever spoken about them by any one? But, if I were only as big as a calf, I would lower the pride of the lions and panthers, and all the world would be talking about me."

Every day our Ass continued to sing this same song to Jupiter, and bothered him so that at last he granted its request, and the Ass became a big beast. But, besides this, it acquired such a savage voice that our long-eared Hercules dismayed the whole forest. "Whatever is that brute? What family does it belong to? It has very long teeth, anyhow, hasn't it? and no end of horns!" At last, nothing else was talked about besides the Ass.

But how did it all end? Before the year was out, every-one had discovered what the Ass really was. Our Ass became proverbial for stupidity, and, ever since that time, Asses have been beasts of burden.

Noble birth and high office are excellent things; but how can they profit a man whose soul is ignoble?

THE CAT AND THE NIGHTINGALE.

A CAT, which had caught a Nightingale, stuck its claws into the poor bird, and, pressing it lovingly, said, "Dear Nightingale, my soul! I hear that you are everywhere renowned for song, and that you are considered equal to the finest singers. My gossip, the Fox, tells me that your voice is so sonorous and wonderful that, at the sound of your entrancing songs, all the shepherds and shepherdesses go out of their wits. I have greatly desired to hear you—don't tremble so, and don't be obstinate, my dear : never fear ; I haven't the least wish to eat you. Only sing me something ; then I will give you your liberty, and release you to wander through the woods and forests.   I don't yield to you in love for music, and I often purr myself to sleep."

Meanwhile our poor Nightingale scarcely breathed under the Cat's claws.

"Well, why don't you begin?" continued the Cat.   "Sing away, dear, however little it may be."

But our songster didn't sing; only uttered a shrill cry.

"What! is it with that you have entranced the forest?" mockingly asked the Cat.   "Where is the clearness, the strength, of which every one talks incessantly?   Such a squeaking I 'm tired of hearing from my kittens.   No; I see that you haven't the least skill in song.   Let 's see how you will taste between my teeth."

And it ate up the poor singer, bones and all.

[This fable, which was published in the year 1824, is said to be intended to depict the painful position which Russian literature occupied at the time, with respect to the Censorship.   During that period of reaction, the press was terribly weighted; and it seemed that, at last, there would be no subjects left of which it was not forbidden to take notice. The censors acted just as they thought fit—altered manuscripts, prohibited books, and stopped the publication of newspapers "till the editors should have knowledge enough to conduct them properly."   It is a pleasure to compare the position which the Russian press holds now, with that which it occupied then.]

THE PEASANT AND THE HORSE.

A PEASANT was sowing oats one day. Seeing that, a young Horse began to reason about it, grumbling to itself.

"A pretty piece of work this, for which he brings such a lot of oats here! And yet they say men are wiser than we are. Can anything possibly be more foolish or ridiculous than to plough up a whole field like this, in order to scatter one's oats over it afterwards to no purpose? Had he given them to me, or to the bay here, or had he even thought fit to fling them to the fowls, it would have all been more like business. Or even if he had hoarded them up, I should have recognised avarice in that. But to fling them uselessly away! No; that is sheer stupidity."

Meanwhile time passed; and in the autumn the oats were garnered, and the Peasant fed this very Horse on them.

Reader, there can be no doubt that you do not approve of the Horse's opinions. But, from the oldest times to our own days, has not man been equally audacious in criticising the designs of Providence, although, in his blind folly, he sees nothing of its means or ends?

THE GNAT AND THE SHEPHERD.

HAVING confided his sheep to the care of his dogs, a Shepherd went to sleep in the shade. Remarking that, a snake glided towards him from under the bushes, brandishing its forked tongue. The Shepherd would have passed away from the world, had not a Gnat taken pity on him, and stung him with all its might. Roused from his slumber, the Shepherd killed the snake. But first, while half awake and half asleep, he hit the Gnat such a slap that the poor thing was utterly done for.

There is no lack of examples of this. If the weak, even with the best intentions, try to open the eyes of the strong, you may expect that they will meet with the same fate as the Gnat.

THE WOLF AND THE CAT.

A WOLF ran out of the forest into a village—not for a visit, but to save its life; for it trembled for its skin. The huntsmen and a pack of hounds were after it. It would fain have rushed in through the first gateway; but there was this unfortunate circumstance in its way, that all the gateways were closed. Our Wolf sees a Cat on a partition fence, and says, pleadingly,

"Vaska, my friend, tell me quickly which of the moujiks here is the kindest, so that I may hide myself from my evil foes? Listen to the cry of the dogs and the terrible sound of the horns! All that noise is actually made in chase of me!"

"Go quickly, and ask Stefan," says Vaska the Cat; "he is a very kind moujik."

"Quite true; only I have torn the skin off one of his sheep."

"Well, then, you can try Demian."

"I'm afraid he's angry with me, too. I carried off one of his kids."

"Run over there, then. Trofim lives there."

"Trofim! I should be afraid of even meeting him. Ever since the spring, he has been threatening me about a lamb."

"Dear me, that's bad! But perhaps Klim will protect you."

"Oh, Vaska, I have killed one of his calves."

"What do I hear, gossip? You've quarrelled with all the village," said Vaska to the Wolf. "What sort of protection can you hope for here? No; our moujiks are not so destitute of sense as to be willing to save you to their own hurt. And, really, you have only yourself to blame. What you have sown, that you must now reap."

THE CANNON AND THE SAILS.

A FIERCE quarrel arose on board a ship between its Cannon and its Sails. Poking their muzzles out of the port-holes, the Cannon thus murmured heavenward :

" O ye gods ! was ever such a thing seen, as that a set of trumpery linen fabrics should have the insolence to set up for being as useful as we are ? In the whole course of our laborious voyage, what have they done ? The moment a breeze begins to blow, they proudly swell out their breasts, carrying themselves above the waves as pompously as if they were really of great importance, but yet do nothing more than show off their airs. But, as for us, we thunder in battles. Is it not due to us that our ship rules the waves ? Do not we carry with us everywhere terror and death ? No ; we do not wish to live any longer with the Sails. We can do everything for ourselves without them. Fly, then, to our aid, mighty Boreas, and quickly tear them into rags."

Boreas heard, and, flying thither, breathed on the sea. Immediately the waters were overcast and turned black, a heavy cloud covered the sky, and the waves ran mountains high. Thunder deafened the ear ; lightning blinded the eye. Boreas roared, and tore the sails into shreds. When nothing was left of them, the tempest ceased. But what followed ?

Deprived of its sails, the ship became a sport to the winds and waves, and drifted about at sea like a log.   And in the first encounter with a hostile vessel, which thundered terrible broadsides along its whole length, our ship, now unable to move, was soon riddled like a sieve, and went down to the bottom like a stone—Cannon and all.

Every state is strong when its elements are wisely balanced. By its Cannon it is terrible to its foes ; but its civil powers play the part of the Sails.

THE EAGLE AND THE BEE.

SEEING how a Bee was busying itself about a flower, an Eagle said to it, with disdain,

"How I pity thee, poor thing, with all thy toil and skill! All through the summer, thousands of thy fellows are moulding honeycomb in the hive. But who will afterwards separate and distinguish the results of thy labour? I must confess, I do not understand what pleasure thou canst take in it. To labour all one's life, and to have in view—what? Why, to die without having achieved distinction, exactly like all the rest. What a difference there is between us! When I spread my sounding pinions, and am borne along near the clouds, I am everywhere a cause of alarm. The birds do not dare to rise from the ground; the shepherds fear to repose beside their well-fed flocks; and the swift does, having seen me, will not venture out into the plains."

But the Bee replies,

"To thee be glory and honour! May Jupiter continue to pour on thee his bounteous gifts! I, however, born to work for the common good, do not seek to make my labour distinguished. But, when I look at our honeycombs, I am consoled by the thought that there are in them a few drops of my own honey."

Fortunate is he, the field of whose labour is conspicuous! He gains added strength from the knowledge that the whole world witnesses his exploits.   But how deserving of respect is he who, in humble obscurity, hopes for neither fame nor honour in return for all his labour, for all his loss of rest —who is animated by this thought only, that he works for the common good!

THE LION.

WHEN the Lion became old and weak, his hard bed began to annoy him. It made his very bones ache; besides, it did not warm him. So he summons his nobles to his side, iong-haired and shaggy wolves and bears, and says,

" Friends, to old bones like mine, my bed has now become intolerably hard. So find out some way, without oppressing either the poor or the rich, to collect fleeces for me, that I may not have to sleep on the bare stones."

" Most illustrious Lion!" answer the grandees, "who would think of grudging you his skin, not to speak of his fleece? And are there but few shaggy beasts among us here? As to stags, hinds, chamois, and goats, they scarcely pay any tribute at all. We will take their fleeces from them at once. They will not be any the worse for that; on the contrary, indeed, they will be all the lighter for it."

This very wise advice was immediately carried out. The Lion could not sufficiently praise the zeal of his friends. But in what had they shown themselves zealous? Only in this, that they caught the poor creatures, and sent them away completely shorn. But they themselves, though they were twice as hirsute, did not contribute so much as a single hair of their own; on the contrary, each of them who happened to be on the spot turned that tribute to good account, and provided himself with a mattress for the winter.

12

THE SWAN, THE PIKE, AND THE CRAB.

A SWAN, a Crab, and a Pike once undertook to draw a load, and all three yoked themselves to it together. They strain away as if they would burst, but the load makes no way. Its weight would have seemed but a light one for them. But the Swan wings its way into the clouds, the Crab crawls backwards, and the Pike flops into the water. Which of them was in the right, and which in the wrong, it is not for us to decide. But the load remains there to the present day.

["From the very commencement of the alliance between France and England for the protection of Turkey," says Mr. Sutherland Edwards, in his "Russians at Home," "Russia asserted—the wish being, of course, father to the assertion —that such a union could never lead to any practical result. In illustration of this idea, a swan, a crab, and a pike, each in its own way a water-animal, were represented in the act of drawing a load—or rather of attempting to do so, for the load remained stationary. Beneath the engraving was printed the fable (by Krilof) from which the idea was taken."]

THE CORN-FLOWER.

A CORN-FLOWER which grew in a retired spot suddenly lost its strength, withered away to little more than half its former size, and, bowing down its head over its stalk, sorrowfully awaited its end. Meanwhile it whispered its complaining to the breeze:

"Ah me! if only the day would soon break, and the shining sun would illumine the fields, perhaps it might revive even me!"

"Why, what a simpleton you are, my friend!" answered a Beetle, which happened to be delving near at hand. "Do you suppose the sun has nothing else to do than to see how you are getting on, and whether you are flourishing or fading? You may be sure that he has neither the time nor the will to do that! If you had flown about like me, and learnt to know the world, you would have perceived that all these meadows, sweeping pastures, and corn-fields owe to him alone both their life and their happiness. He warms the huge oaks and cedars by his heat, and he richly clothes with wondrous beauty the sweet-smelling flowers. But those flowers are utterly different from you. So precious are they and so beautiful, that Time himself pities them as he mows

12—2

them down.   But as for you, you are neither splendid nor
fragrant, so don't annoy the sun by your importunity! Make
up your mind that he won't spare you a ray, and cease to
strive after what cannot be got.   Hold your tongue, and
wither !"

But the sun arose, illuminating all nature, and widely
scattering its beams over the kingdom of Flora.   And the
poor Corn-flower, which had begun to fade away in the night,
was brought back to life by its celestial regard.

O ye upon whom Fate has conferred high dignity, take
as an example for yourselves this sun of which I have spoken.
Wherever his light falls, there it benefits all alike, whether it
be a cedar or a blade of grass, and there it leaves behind it
joy and happiness; wherefore, also, its image glitters in the
hearts of all, as shines in Eastern crystals a limpid light, and
all things that be invoke blessings upon it.

[In 1823 Krilof was for some time seriously ill.   When
the Empress Maria Fedorovna heard of his attack, she told
his friends to send him to Pavlovsk, where she was staying
at that time, saying, "He will recover quicker under my
charge."   Accordingly he went there as soon as he became
convalescent, and remained there for some time.   Before he
left he composed the poem of the Corn-flower, and placed
it one day in an album belonging to the Empress, which he
found lying in the "Pavilion of Roses."]

PARNASSUS.

AFTER the Gods had been driven out of Greece, and when their domains were being divided among mortals, a certain man had Parnassus itself allotted to him. The new landlord turned out a number of Asses to graze on it. Now these Asses had learnt, somehow or other, that the Muses used to live there in former times; so they said,

"It wasn't for nothing that we were turned out on Parnassus. It is evident that the world is tired of the Muses, and it wants us to take to singing here."

Then one exclaimed,

"Look sharp there, and don't lose heart. I will lead off: mind you are not behindhand. We must not be timid, friends. Rather will we lift up our voices louder than those of the Nine Sisters, rendering our herd illustrious. And we will form our own choir, and, in order that our confraternity may not be disconcerted, we will establish among ourselves such a regulation as this—that we will not admit upon Parnassus any but those in whose voices the asinine charm is to be found."

The Asses approved of the beautiful and artistically-constructed speech of the Ass, and the novel choir set up a

screech that sounded as if a train of waggons were rolling
along on a thousand unoiled wheels.   But how did the
varied beauty of the singing end?   Why, the landlord,
losing all patience, drove them away from Parnassus into
his stable.

If it will not hurt the feelings of the uncultivated, I
should like to quote the ancient saw :

> " To a head that is empty no art can add brains :
> Though you place it in office—it empty remains."

[This fable is supposed to refer to the downfall of what
was called the " English " Ministry in Russia, after the meeting which took place at Tilsit between Alexander I. and
Napoleon.   When Alexander came to the throne he dis-
placed most of the old Ministers, and gave their portfolios
to young men who shared his own liberal ideas.   They held
office for five years.   Then came the change in Alexander's
policy, which drove them out, so that by the end of 1807 not
one of them was left in power.   Krilof, as a Conservative,
and an admirer of the old school of politicians formed under
Catherine II., was delighted at the fall of the " Young-Rus-
sian " Ministry.]

THE LINNET AND THE HEDGEHOG.

A TIMID Linnet, a lover of solitude, was chirruping away to itself one morning at daybreak, but not because it wanted to be applauded — and, indeed, there could not have been any reason for applauding it; its song flowed from it involuntarily.

But, see! in all his blaze of glory resplendent Phœbus rose from out of the waves, seeming to bring life to all things along with him; and to welcome him, a chorus of clear-voiced nightingales made the dense woods resound with song. Our Linnet became silent.

"But you, my friend, why don't you sing?" tauntingly asked the Hedgehog.

"Because my voice is not fit for worthily extolling Phœbus," answered the poor Linnet, through its tears. "With a feeble voice I cannot venture to sing of Phœbus."

So I, too, grieve, and complain that Pindar's lyre did not fall to my lot. Had that been the case I would have sung of Alexander.

[This little poem derives its main interest from the fact that Krilof refers in it to himself.   When Alexander I. was on his way back to Russia after the occupation of Paris, the poets of the day broke out into a chorus of congratulatory song.   Krilof's friends advised him to write a poem on the subject.   But about a month before Alexander returned, Krilof paid a visit to the Empress-Dowager, Maria Fedorovna, and recited to her this little fable.]

THE WOOD AND THE FIRE.

ONE winter day the remains of a Fire were smouldering in a Wood, forgotten there, no doubt, by some chance travellers. Hour by hour the Fire grew weaker. No fresh fuel being supplied to it, our Fire almost ceased to burn, and, seeing its end near at hand, thus spoke to the Wood:

"Tell me, dear Wood, why your fate is so hard that not a leaflet can be seen on you, and you are freezing in utter bareness?"

"Because," replied the Wood, "I cannot put forth buds or foliage in the winter-time, when the snow is over all."

"A mere trifle!" continues the Fire. "Only ally yourself with me. I will assist you. I am the Sun's brother; and, in the winter season, I work miracles as much as the Sun. Ask about the fire in hothouses: inside them, during the winter, when the snow falls and the storm-wind is blowing without, everything is either blossoming or ripening, and that is all due to me. Self-praise is unbecoming, and I detest bragging; but as far as strength is concerned I will in

nowise yield to the Sun.   However proudly he may have
shone here, he has gone to his bed without doing any harm
to the snow.   But around me, only see how the snow has
melted.   So if you want to grow green in winter, just as
in spring and summer, grant me a little corner of your
space."

See, the matter is agreed about: already, there, in the
wood, have the smouldering embers become a fire; and
that fire does not sleep.   It runs along the branches and
among the twigs.   A black smoke soars in wreaths to the
clouds, and a fierce flame suddenly enwraps the whole Wood.
All perishes utterly; and there, where upon sultry days the
traveller used to find a refuge in the shade, only blackened
stumps stand out a little from the ground.

Not that there is anything to wonder at in this, for how
can wood and fire be friends?

THE TITMOUSE.

A TITMOUSE made assault upon the sea, boasting that it would burn the sea up. Immediately there went abroad through all the world much talk about that. Fear seized upon the inhabitants of Neptune's metropolis. The birds flew in troops, and the beasts ran down together from the forests, to see in what manner the ocean would take fire, and whether it would burn furiously. It is even said, on the authority of the feathered tribe, that the human haunters of festal tables were among the first to appear on the shore, all provided with spoons, so as to enjoy so rich a fish soup as not even the most liberal of contractors had ever given to Government officials.

They swarm around. Each one marvels at the prodigy beforehand, and, in utter silence, fixing his eyes upon the sea, awaits the result. Only at times will one of them whisper, "There, it is going to boil! Look! it will begin to burn in a minute!"

Not a bit of it! the sea does not burn. But at all events doesn't it boil? It does not even boil. Well, then, how did these stupendous projects end? Why, the Titmouse had to fly away home in disgrace. The Titmouse had made a noise in the world, but it had not set the sea on fire.

THE MONKEYS.

WHEN folks imitate discreetly, there is no wonder in their gaining by the process. But, as to indiscreet imitation—Heaven protect us! what a terrible thing that is!

I will give you an illustration of this, brought from a far-off land.

All who have seen monkeys know how fond they are of imitating everything. Well, one day, in Africa, where monkeys are numerous, there was a whole troop of them sitting on the boughs and branches of a thick tree, and looking aside at a hunter, watching how he rolled about on the grass among his nets. Each one gave her neighbour a quiet nudge in the ribs, and they all began to whisper to each other—

"Just look at the fine fellow! Really it would seem that there is no end to his frolics! How he rolls over and over —turns himself inside out, and coils himself up into a ball so that one can't see either his hands or his feet! It is true that we are already well skilled in everything, but such science as that has never even been seen among us before. Sister beauties! it would not be a bad idea for us to imitate it! That fellow seems to have amused himself enough; perhaps he will go away, and then we will at once——"

See, he really has gone away and left the nets to them.

"There now!" they say, "ought we to lose any time? Let's go and make an experiment."

The beauties descend. For the dear guests a quantity of nets have been spread down below. They begin to turn head over heels, to roll about, to envelope and entangle themselves in the toils. They cry—they squeal! their joy is at its height. But see! when it comes to extricating themselves from the nets, it is a bad business for them! Their entertainer has been all along on the watch, and, when he sees the time has come, he provides himself with sacks and walks up to his guests. Fain would they take to flight, but not one of them can get free now; and so, one after the other, they are all made prisoners.

THE DUCAT.

IS civilization profitable? Profitable!—that is not the question. But we often give the name of civilization to luxury's seductions, and even to demoralization. Therefore you must pay close attention, so that, when you rid people of their superficial coarseness, you may not at the same time rob them of their good qualities, enfeeble their souls, spoil their morals, deprive them of their simplicity, and, having given them in exchange merely an empty brilliance, burden them with infamy instead of good repute.

About this sacred truth one might make a whole volume of serious sermons, but serious speaking does not befit every one; so, half in jest, I am going to prove it to you by means of a fable.

A Peasant, a thorough blockhead (there are plenty of such people everywhere) found a Ducat lying on the ground. The Ducat was dusty and dirty, but three double handfuls of five-kopeck pieces were ready to be given to the Peasant in exchange for it.

"Stop a bit!" thinks the Peasant: "they'll give me twice as much presently. I've hit on such a plan that they'll try to get it from me with both hands."

Hereupon, having taken sand, gravel, chalk, and brick-dust, our Moujik sets to work, and with all his might chafes the Ducat against the gravel, grinds it with sand and brick-dust, and rubs it with chalk.

Well, to speak briefly, he wants to make it shine like fire, and like actual fire the Ducat begins to gleam. Only—its weight diminished, and so the Ducat lost its ancient value.

[During the early years of the reign of Alexander I., a great deal was done in the name of enlightenment. It was proposed to found educational establishments all over Russia. Three Universities were reformed, and two were completely reconstituted ; three High Schools were founded, together with twenty-six Gymnasia and eighty District Schools. A thirst for instruction began to make itself felt among all the classes of the Russian people. The rich subscribed liberally ; even the poor "laid their mite on the altar of national enlightenment." Between the years 1800 and 1812 more than three hundred educational establishments of different kinds were opened. In the eventful year 1812 itself no less than fifty-one new schools were made available.

Even the peasants contributed towards the funds which were subscribed for the new colleges and schools. But in these new schools French teachers exercised great influence, and Krilof detested that influence as being hostile to patriotic feeling. Hence arose his want of sympathy with that desire for education which for a time seemed likely to become universal.]

THE TRAVELLERS AND THE DOGS.

ONE evening two friends were walking along, and carrying on a sensible conversation, when suddenly from the threshold of a gateway a yard-dog began to bark at them. After it began a second, then two or three others, and in another moment half a hundred dogs had run together from all the courtyards. Already was one of the travellers on the point of picking up a stone, when the other one said to him,

"Hold hard, brother! You won't prevent the dogs from barking; you will only provoke the pack all the more. Let's go straight on. I know their nature better."

And, in fact, they had only gone some fifty paces when the dogs gradually began to calm down, and at last they could not be heard at all.

The envious can look at nothing without setting up a howl at it. But you go your own way. They may continue barking for awhile—but they will leave off.

[A recent critic, M. Fleury, has called attention to the resemblance between this fable and the following, extracted from the preface to Voltaire's "Alzire": "Un Voyageur était importuné dans son chemin du bruit des cigales; il s'arrêta pour les tuer; il n'en vint pas à bout, et ne fit que s'écarter de sa route. Il n'avait qu' a continuer paisible-ment son voyage; les cigales seraient mortes d'elles-mêmes au bout de huit jours."

But Krilof's fable has a wider signification than that of Voltaire, which refers mainly to literary critics.]

THE PEASANT AND THE SNAKE.

A SNAKE came and asked a Peasant to take it into his house. Not to live there idly without working — no, it wanted to look after his children. Bread is sweetest when it is earned by labour.

" I know," it says, " what a bad name snakes have got among you men—how they are all supposed to be of the very worst character. From the remotest times rumour has asserted that gratitude is unknown to them, that they know neither friendship nor relationship, and that they devour even their own little ones. All that may be true, but I am not one of that sort. Not only have I never bitten anybody in my life, but I have such a loathing for everything that is hurtful, that I would have had my sting pulled out of me if I could only have been sure that I could live without one. To speak briefly : of all snakes I am the best. Judge, then, how fond I shall be of your children ! "

" Even supposing all that isn't all lies," answers the Peasant, " yet it 's quite impossible for me to take you in. As soon as one specimen of the kind got to be liked among us, a hundred bad snakes would come crawling in after the one good one, and would be the ruin of all our children here.

Indeed I fancy, my dear creature, that it is impossible for you and me to live on good terms together, for, according to my ideas, the very best of snakes is not good enough for even the devil himself."

Fathers, do you understand what I am thinking about just now?

[After the campaign of 1812, the *Vuimorozki*,* as they were called—the remnants of the *Grande Armée*—were dispersed about Russia, and very kindly treated, being made much of at all convivial meetings, and readily accepted as tutors, sometimes as husbands. Against all this Krilof uttered several protests, one of which is embodied in the present fable.]

---

* The spiritual essence obtained from frozen wine, etc.

THE FLOWERS.

AT the open window of a sumptuous apartment, arranged in vases of many-coloured porcelain, a number of Artificial Flowers waved proudly on their wire stalks—real flowers standing beside them the while—and exhibited their charms to universal admiration.

But, see! a shower has begun to fall. The taffeta Flowers straightway adjure Jupiter, asking if the rain cannot be stopped, abusing and defaming it in every way.

"O Jupiter," they pray, "do put a stop to this shower! What good is there in it? what on earth can be worse than it is? Why, see! walking in the streets is impossible, for it has turned them into nothing but mud and puddles."

But Jupiter gave no heed to their idle prayer, and the shower had it all its own way, dispelled the great heat, and made the air cool. All nature revived, and the verdure on every side seemed to spring up anew.

Then, among other things, the real flowers in the window expanded in all their beauty, fresher for the rain, softer and more fragrant. But by that time the Artificial Flowers, poor things! had lost all their beauty, and they were thrown into the yard as rubbish.

Real talents are not angry with criticism: it cannot injure their charms.

It is only the false flowers that fear the rain.

SPREADING from a spark into a conflagration, a Fire, in the dead of midnight, rushed with furious impetuosity through a pile of buildings.

Meanwhile a Diamond, which had been lost in the universal alarm, faintly glimmered through the dust of the road in which it lay.

"How thoroughly art thou, in spite of all thy play of light, annihilated in my presence !" said the Fire. "And how practised must be that sight which can distinguish thee, at a little distance, from either a bit of glass or a drop of water in which my light or that of the sun shines reflected ! not to speak of how much damage is done to thee by anything that falls upon thee—any trifle, a mere scrap of ribbon. How often, for instance, does a single hair which has wound itself about thee dim thy brilliance ! Not so easily is my radiance to be eclipsed when I encompass a building in my wrath. See how I despise all the efforts people are making against me ! How I devour with a crackling all that I encounter ! while my glare, playing upon the clouds, brings fear upon all the land around !"

"It is true that my light is really but a poor one compared with thine," answered the Diamond. "But I am harmless. None can accuse me of having injured any one, and to envy alone is my light distasteful. But thou shinest, thou flashest, only by means of that which destroys; therefore, see how all, uniting their whole strength, strive that thou mayest be extinguished as soon as possible. And the more furiously thou blazest, the quicker, perhaps, dost thou draw to thy end."

Meanwhile the people strove with all their might to put out the Fire. By the morning nothing was left of it but smoke and stench. But the Diamond was soon recovered, and it became the chief ornament of the royal crown.

"HOW comes it," said to a River a neighbouring Pond, "that one never looks at you without finding your waters always in movement? Is it possible, sister dear, that you do not grow tired? Besides, I see that you are almost always supporting either heavily-laden ships or long lines of timber-rafts; I say nothing at present about boats and barges: their number is infinite! When will you have done with such a life? I should really dry up from vexation if mine were like it.

"But, in comparison with yours, how pleasant is my lot! It is true that I am not known to fame. I do not meander across a whole sheet of the map; no dulcimer player twangs out praises in my honour: all that is, in reality, mere nonsense. But I, on my soft and slimy banks, repose in tranquil indulgence, like a fine lady on cushions of down. And not only have I no ships or rafts to fear, but I do not even know what the weight of a boat is. Nay, more, I think it a great event if a leaf, which the breeze has wafted to me, undulates on my waters. What equivalent could be offered for a life so free from cares? Left behind, unruffled by the winds from whatever quarter they may blow, I know no movement, but look on, as in a dream, at the world's anxieties, and philosophize the while."

"But, while philosophizing, do you bear in mind this law," replied the River, "that only by movement can water preserve its freshness? If I have become a great river, it has been because, spurning rest, I obey that law. Therefore is it that, year after year, I benefit by the abundance and purity of my waters, and gain honour and glory. It may be, too, that for ages to come I shall still flow on, when you will no longer exist even in memory, and all mention of you will have utterly come to an end."

The words of the River were fulfilled: to this day it still flows on. But the poor Pond, becoming every year less liquid, and more and more choked up with thick ooze, turned mouldy, produced a crop of sedge, and finally dried up.

THE EAGLE AND THE MOLE.

AN Eagle and his mate flew into a deep forest, and determined to make it their permanent abode. So they chose an oak, lofty and wide-spreading, and began to build themselves a nest on the top of it, hoping there to rear their young in the summer.

A Mole, who heard about all this, plucked up courage enough to inform the Eagles that the oak was not a proper dwelling-place for them; that it was almost entirely rotten at the root, and was likely soon to fall, and that therefore the Eagles ought not to make their nest upon it.

But is it becoming that an Eagle should accept advice coming from a Mole in a hole? Where then would be the glory of an Eagle having such keen eyes? And how comes it that Moles dare to meddle in the affairs of the King of Birds?

So, saying very little to the Mole, whose counsel he despised, the Eagle set to work quickly—and the King soon got ready the new dwelling for the Queen.

All goes well, and now the Eagles have little ones. But what happens? One day, when at early dawn the Eagle is hastening back from the chase, bringing a rich breakfast to

his family, as he drops down from the sky he sees—his oak
has fallen, and has crushed beneath it his mate and his little
ones !

"Wretched creature that I am !" he cries, anguish blotting
out from him the light; "for my pride has Fate so terribly
punished me, and because I gave no heed to wise counsel.
But could one expect that wise counsel could possibly come
from a miserable Mole?"

Then from its hole the Mole replies :

"Had not you despised me, you would have remembered
that I burrow within the earth, and that, as I live among the
roots, I can tell with certainty whether a tree be sound or
no."

THE STARLING.

A CERTAIN Starling learnt, in early life, to sing as like a goldfinch as if it had been born a goldfinch itself. The whole forest was enlivened by its sportive little lay, and the dear Starling was the theme of universal praise.

Any other bird would have been content with such honours. But our Starling heard the nightingale being praised. Our Starling, to its sorrow, became jealous.

"Just wait a little, my friends," it thinks; "I will sing in the nightingale's style too, and every bit as well."

And it really did begin singing, only it was in a style quite different from anything else. It squeaked, it growled, it whimpered like a kid, and, without the least reason for doing so, mewed like a kitten. To be brief, its singing made all the other birds take to flight.

Well, my dear Starling! what have you gained by that? Better sing a goldfinch's song well, than a nightingale's badly.

"DEAR friend," cried a young Sapling to a peasant, whom it saw carrying an axe, "please clear away the forest around me. I cannot grow comfortably, nor can I see the light of the sun; my roots have not space enough, and the breezes are not at liberty to sport around me; such arches has it thought fit to weave above me. If it were not for its impeding my growth I should become the ornament of the neighbourhood in a year, and all the valley would be covered by my shade. But as it is I am thin and frail, almost like a withered branch."

The peasant took to his axe and rendered service to the Tree as to a friend. Around the sapling a great space was cleared, but not long did its triumph last! At one time it was parched by the sun, at another it was knocked about by hail or rain, and at last it was snapped in two by the wind.

"Fool!" then said to it a Snake, "have you not brought your misfortune upon yourself? If you had grown up, hidden by the forest, neither heat nor storm would have been able to hurt you. The old trees would have protected you; and if a time had come when their season was past and they disappeared, then you, in your turn, would have so flourished, would have become so strongly built and firmly rooted, that your present misfortune would never have happened to you, and you would, perhaps, have been able to encounter even the hurricane.

THE PEASANT AND THE FOX.

"TELL me, gossip, how is it you have such a passion for stealing fowls?" said a Peasant to a Fox he happened to meet. "I declare I feel quite sorry for you. Listen now; we are alone here, and I will tell you the whole truth. In your way of living there really is not a grain of good to be seen—not to mention that theft is a sin and a shame, and that all the world curses you; and there never is a single day on which you are not afraid, by way of payment for your dinner or supper, of leaving your skin behind you in the poultry-yard. Now, are all the fowls in the world worth this?"

"Who could find such a life endurable?" answered the Fox. "I am so disgusted with everything in it· that I find my very food distasteful; and if you only knew how pure I am in heart! But what is one to do? I have wants; I have children. Besides, dear gossip, the thought sometimes comes into my head that, perhaps, I am not the only one in the world who lives by stealing, and yet that profession is to me just as it were a sharp knife stuck into me."

" Very good," says the Peasant. " If you are really not telling lies, I will save you from sinning, and provide you with honest food. Hire yourself to me to guard my poultry-yard against the foxes. Who but a fox is likely to know all foxish tricks? And in return for this you shall want for nothing: in my service you will roll like a cheese in butter."

The bargain was struck, and from that very hour the Fox went upon guard. The Fox led a life of abundance at the Peasant's. The Fox grew fuller, the Fox grew fatter, but the Fox did not grow more honest. Food which had not been stolen soon became distasteful to him, and our gossip ended his service by taking advantage of an unusually dark night, and throttling every fowl his dear friend possessed.

THE GARDENER AND THE PHILOSOPHER.

ONE spring, a Gardener took to digging away among his beds as vigorously as if he were in hopes of digging up a treasure. A mettlesome workman was the Moujik, and stout and fresh to look at. Before long he had prepared some fifty beds for cucumbers alone.

Next door to him lived an amateur of gardens, both kitchen and flower—a very fine talker, a friend of Nature, as he called himself, a philosopher of the superficial school, one who chatted away about gardens from book-knowledge only.

One day he took it into his head to look after his own garden, and he, too, determined to rear cucumbers, and in the meantime he thus flouted his neighbour:

" Sweat away, neighbour, as much as you like, but my work will leave yours far behind, and by the side of my garden yours will look like a desert. Yes, to tell the truth, I have often been quite astounded at seeing that that miserable little garden of yours gets on at all. How is it you have not been ruined before now? I suppose you have never paid the least attention to science?"

" Never had the time," was the neighbour's answer. " Industry, practice, a pair of arms—these are all the sciences I have. But just as they are, God gives me bread with them."

"Clodhopper! Do you dare to set yourself up against science?"

"No, master; don't go twisting my words askew like that. If you invent anything clever, I'll always be ready to copy you."

"Well, well! we shall see; just let's wait till summer——"

"But, master, isn't this the time for taking the matter in hand? I've already begun sowing and planting, but you haven't even dug over your beds yet."

"Why, no, I haven't done any digging yet for want of leisure. I've been spending all my time in reading, trying to find out from my books whether I should dig the beds with a spade, or whether it would not be better to use one of the two kinds of ploughs, and if so, which of the two? But the season is not going to pass away just yet."

"Not from you, perhaps; but it won't be much inclined to wait for me," said the Gardener, turning away and taking to his spade again.

The Philosopher went home and began reading, making extracts, inquiring, and digging away in his library and in his garden, always at work from morn till eve. Scarcely had he finished one piece of work, hardly had anything come up in the beds, when he would find some fresh discovery in the newspapers. Straightway he would dig up everything, transplant everything, on another plan, to a new tune.

What, then, was the result of all this? Everything the Gardener had sown came up and ripened. His affairs went well, and brought him in profit. But as for the Philosopher —not a single cucumber had he.

THE DOG.

A GENTLEMAN had a dog that was given to thieving. And yet there was nothing it stood in need of. Any other dog in such a kind of life would have been happy and contented, and would never have dreamt of stealing. But this one had such a mania for it that whenever it got hold of a piece of meat it instantly bolted with it.

In spite of all the pains his master gave himself, he could not get on with it, until at last a friend interfered and helped him with this piece of advice:

"Listen," he said. "Athough you are severe, it seems, yet you only accustom your dog to steal, inasmuch as you always let him keep his stolen morsel. But suppose you beat him less in future, only take away from him what he has stolen."

Scarcely had the dog experienced the effect of this wise counsel when—the dog gave up stealing.

[This fable, like that of "The Bear among the Bees," refers to the corruption which used to be so prevalent in Russian official circles. In the dog of the one story and the bear of the other, individual functionaries of evil repute were in all probability represented, but their real names are unknown.]

THE APE.

A PEASANT at the dawn of day went toiling over his
bit of ground behind his plough. So hard did our
peasant toil that the sweat poured off him like hail. Our
Moujik was a thorough workman, and therefore everybody
who went past called out to him, " Well done! Good luck
to you!"

This made an Ape jealous. Praise is tempting: how can
one help longing for it? So the Ape took it into his head
to work, got hold of a log, and just did plague himself over
it. The Ape's mouth becomes full of trouble. Now he lifts
up the log, and now embraces it, first this way, then that;

11—2

now he drags it along, now he rolls it about. The sweat
runs off the poor creature in a stream. At last, groaning
and gasping, he can scarcely draw his breath.

And yet, in spite of all this, he does not hear a soul give
him an atom of praise. And no wonder, my dear! You
take a world of pains, but what you do is utterly useless.

[This fable is suspiciously like one of Sumarokof's, called
"The Ploughman and the Monkey," in which the man gets
praised, while the monkey, who is toiling away with a stone,
gets nothing but a scolding, and cannot make out why.]

THE CASK.

A CERTAIN man asked a friend to lend him a cask for two or three days. Now, in friendship, a readiness to oblige is a holy thing. You see, if the matter had been one of money, that would have been quite another question. In that case friendship would have been beside the mark, and it would have been possible to refuse. But as to lending a cask—why shouldn't one?

When it had been returned, they began carrying water in it again. And everything would have been all right about it if it had not been for this—that a spirit merchant had used it for keeping brandy in, and it had become so saturated with the spirit in a couple of days, that it communicated a flavour of brandy to everything that was put into it — to kvass or beer, whichever had been brewed, or even to eatables.

Almost an entire year did its owner bother himself about it : at one time scalded it, at another hung it out to air in the breeze. But let him pour into it what he liked, the spirituous flavour would not go out of it a bit. And so, at last, he was obliged to part with the cask.

Fathers ! try not to forget this fable.   If in his young days
one of us has ever happened to be steeped in the current of
a hurtful teaching, then in all his actions and behaviour afterwards, whatever he may be in words, there will always be
perceptible a kind of after-taste of it.

[This fable seems only an expansion of the lines of Horace :

" Nunc adbibe puro
Pectore verba, puer, nunc te melioribus offer.
Quo semel est imbuta recens servabit odorem
Testa diu."—*Epist.* I. 2.

An idea which was expanded by St. Jerome as follows :

" Difficulter eraditur, quod rudes animi perbiberunt. Lana-
rum conchylia quis in pristinum colorem revocet ?   Rudis
testa diu et saporem retinet et odorem, quo primum imbuta
est."—*Epist. ad Lætam.*

In a quaint version published in 1630, the passage is thus
translated :

" That is hardly scraped out, which young unfashioned
mindes have drunke in. Who shall be able to reduce purple
woolls to the former whitenes? A new vessell long retaynes
both the odour and taste, whereof it received the first impression."

Krilof felt strongly on the subject of education, to which
he devoted three of his fables: "The Peasant and the Snake,"
"The Cask," and "The Education of the Lion," besides
two comedies—the "Fashions Shop," and the "Lesson for
Daughters."   In his "Spirit Post" he says: "A hundred

years ago people educated their children themselves, caring only about their being honest, brave in war, and firm under misfortune. Parents tried to be good in those days in order to set a good example to their children. People were not eloquent, but they spoke truths which stood in no need of eloquence. But now it is thought that a man cannot be a good citizen unless he can dance, play cards, talk French, and chatter away all the day long. And for all that French tutors are needed."

Krilof hated these French tutors, for he remained firmly attached to old-fashioned views about religion and politics. At the time when the fable was written, in the year 1814, the Empire had been greatly influenced by the teachings of the Mysticists on the one hand and the Freethinkers on the other. After 1812, so many Frenchmen remained in Russia as teachers, that French ideas spread widely among the younger Russians of the upper class.

> "Græcia capta ferum victorem cepit et artes
> Intulit agresti Latio."]

THE NOBLEMAN AND THE PHILOSOPHER.

A NOBLEMAN chatting with a Sage during an idle hour about one thing and the other, said,

"Tell me, you who thoroughly know the world, and read the hearts of people like a book, how is it that, whenever we lay the foundation of an assembly or a learned society, we scarcely have time to take a look around us, before the blockheads manage to worm themselves in among the first comers? Is it possible that absolutely no remedy exists against them?"

"I think not," replied the Sage. "The fate of learned societies is the same, between ourselves, as that of houses made of wood."

"How so?"

"Why, this way. I have just now finished building one for myself. Its proprietors have not yet moved into it, but the crickets have ever so long ago taken up their quarters in it."

THE HORSE AND ITS RIDER.

A CERTAIN Cavalier had so schooled his horse, that he could do whatever he liked with it. He scarcely made any use of the reins : the Horse obeyed his mere word.

"There's no use in bridling such horses," said its master one day. "Upon my word, I've hit on a capital idea !"

And riding out afield he unbridled the horse.

When it felt itself free, the horse at first only increased its pace a little, and, tossing its head and shaking its mane, it speeded with playful gait as if to amuse its rider.

But when it remarked how weak was now the power that used to control it, the mettlesome horse soon began to follow its own will. Its blood boiled, its eyes glowed. No longer listening to the voice of its rider, it whirled him along at full speed right across the open country.

In vain did our unfortunate rider attempt with trembling hands to throw the bridle over its head. The horse only became the fiercer, and away it tore, until at last it flung its rider far from its back. Then away, like a whirling storm-wind, it rushed, blind to the light of heaven, not seeing where it went, until it fell headlong into a ravine, and was knocked to pieces.

"My poor horse!" said its rider, when he heard of its death. "It was I who brought about thy misfortune. If I had not taken off thy bridle, I should certainly have been able to guide thee. Then thou wouldst not have thrown me, nor wouldst thou have died so pitiful a death!"

How alluring is liberty! But for a people it is no less destructive, unless reasonable bounds are set to it.

[It has been supposed that Krilof meant this fable to apply to the revolutionary agitation in Russia, which began to manifest itself after the war with Napoleon, and which went on increasing till its unfortunate outbreak in 1825. But it was written before that agitation commenced, the original MS. being dated May 12, 1814, and it is probable that Krilof, when he composed it, was thinking only of the French Revolution.

There is a poem by Derjavine called the *Kolesnitsa,* or "Chariot," to which this fable bears a strong likeness.]

THE GOOD FOX.

A SPORTSMAN killed a redcap one spring. Would that the evil he wrought had ended with her life! But, no—after hers three more lives had to be lost. The sportsman had made orphans of her three little ones, poor creatures! Only just out of the shell, feeble and ignorant, they suffered from cold and hunger, calling in vain upon their dam with plaintive cry.

"How can one help grieving at the sight of these little ones, and whose heart does not ache for them?" Thus were the neighbouring birds addressed by a Fox, who was sitting on a bit of stone opposite the nest of the orphans. "Don't leave these young creatures unassisted, my dear friends. If you will only bring the poor little darlings a tiny grain apiece, if each of you will only add to their dear little nest ever so small a straw, you will thereby save their lives. And what is more holy than a good deed?

"O cuckoo dear! just see how thou art moulting! Would it not be as well for thee to allow thyself to be plucked a little, and to give thy feathers to garnish their little bed? Really, thou art now losing them uselessly.

"O lark! suppose that, instead of turning and tumbling about high up in the air, thou wert sometimes to look for food in the corn-field and the meadow, and to share it with the orphans.

"O turtle-dove! thy young ones have now grown up; they are able to procure their own food now, so it is possible for thee to fly from thy own nest, and take their mother's place over these little ones, leaving God to watch over thy own offspring.

"O swallow! suppose thou wert to catch flies, so as to make the fare of the orphans a little more dainty.

"And thou, dear nightingale, thou knowest how all things feel the charm of thy voice. Why shouldst thou not lull the little ones to rest by thy sweet song, while the zephyr rocks them in their nest?

"By such kindness, I am convinced, ye would make up to them for their sad loss. Only listen to me—we will prove that there are kind hearts in the forest, and that——"

As the Fox was saying these words, all three of the poor little birds, prevented by their hunger from keeping still, fell down on the ground just in front of him.

What did their kind friend do? Gobbled them up immediately, without finishing his sermon!

[This fable bears a good deal of resemblance to Florian's "*Renard qui prêche*," which was translated by Dmitrief under the title of "The Preaching Fox." Kenevich thinks that it relates to the subscriptions which were organized in 1814—

the year in which it appeared—for the benefit of the families which had been ruined during the French invasion. Some of the persons who got up these subscriptions, or who wrote letters about them to the papers, were supposed to be actuated by not quite disinterested motives.]

THE COMMUNAL ASSEMBLY.

THE Wolf asked the Lion to appoint him inspector over the Sheep. Thanks to the pains taken by his gossip the Fox, a friendly word had been spoken about him to the Lioness.

But, inasmuch as wolves have a bad name in the world, and in order that it might not be said that the Lion shows favour to persons, therefore orders were given to the whole animal kingdom to meet together in a general assembly, and there to inquire on all sides what any one knew, good or bad, about the Wolf.

The order was obeyed. The animals were all convoked, and their voices were gathered befittingly in the assembly.

Against the Wolf not a word was said. So the Wolf was appointed to preside over the sheep-fold.

But the Sheep? What did they say? Of course they were at the assembly?

Well, it seems they weren't. Somehow the Sheep had been forgotten.

And yet it was they whose opinion was wanted the most.

THE TWO CASKS.

THERE go two casks. One full of wine, the other empty. See how silently, at a mere foot's pace, the first drags itself along; but the other flies past at a gallop, with a sound of thunder from its banging along the road, and a pillar of dust above it. Hearing it afar off, the passer-by hurries aside in fear.

But, noisy as that cask may be, there is not as much use in it as in the other.

There is little real good in a man who never ceases telling every one about his own performances. He who is really great in deeds is generally sparing of words. A great man makes a noise only by what he does, shaping in silence his firm resolve.

THE FALSE ACCUSATION.

THERE lived in the East a certain Brahmin, who, though fervently orthodox in his words, was not so in his way of life. Even among Brahmins there are hypocrites: but that is beside the mark. This only is to the point, that he alone of all the brotherhood was a man of that kind. All the rest were men of holy lives, and—what was, above all things, distasteful to our friend—their chief was of an exceedingly strict character, so that no one could ever venture to break the rules.

But our Brahmin did not lose courage. A fast-day comes, but he meditates as to whether it may not be possible for him to obtain a secret indulgence for something luscious. Having laid his hands on an egg, and having waited till midnight, he lights a candle and sets to work to cook his egg above it. Steadily does he turn the egg above the flame, never takes his eyes off it, and already swallows it in anticipation. Meanwhile he thinks about his chief, chuckling to himself,

"You won't find me out, my long-bearded friend! This egg anyhow I shall eat with relish."

But at this moment the chief suddenly enters the Brahmin's

cell, and, at the sight of such a sin, asks in a terrible voice what the Brahmin has to say for himself.

The proof is there before his eyes: it is too late to deny the fact.

"Forgive me my sin! holy father, forgive!" the Brahmin implores between his tears. "I cannot tell what led me into this temptation. Ah, yes! it was the accursed Evil One who put the idea into my head."

But at that moment a little demon cried out from behind the stove:

"What a shame it is to be always calumniating us! Why, I myself have just been taking a lesson from you; for, I assure you, this is the first time I ever saw how to cook eggs at a candle."

THE FROG AND JUPITER.

A FROG which lived in a swamp at the foot of a hill, changed its quarters one spring, and went up the hill. There it found a muddy corner in a little hollow, and set up a small abode, like a tiny Paradise, amidst grass and in the shade of a bush.

But it did not long enjoy itself there. The summer came, and the heat with it, and the Croaker's country seat became so dry that the flies wandered about over it without wetting their feet.

"O ye gods!" prayed the Frog from its hole, "don't destroy poor me, but send a deluge over the face of the earth as high as this hill, so that the water may never dry up in these my domains!"

The Frog went on complaining incessantly, and at last took to upbraiding Jupiter, and saying that there was neither sense nor pity in him.

"Idiot!" cried Jupiter, who evidently was not in a bad humour just then; "what pleasure can you find in croaking such nonsense? Why should I drown mankind for your whims? Wouldn't it be better for you to crawl down to your swamp again?"

THE EAGLE AND THE FOWLS.

WISHING to enjoy a bright day to the utmost, an Eagle soared into the upper regions of the air, and floated about in the birthplace of the thunderbolt. At length, having come down from those cloudy heights, the King of Birds settled on a kiln for drying corn, and there took breath. To be sure it was not a becoming perch for an eagle. But kings have their whims. Perhaps he wanted to do honour to the kiln, or else there was no object near, no oak, no granite rock, on which he could be seated as became his rank. What his fancy may have been I know not,

15—2

but only this, that he remained sitting there but a short time, and then flew across to another kiln.

Having seen that, a tufted brood-hen thus chattered to her gossip :

"Why are eagles so highly honoured? It can't be for their flight, my sweet neighbour. Why, upon my word, if I felt inclined, I also could fly across from kiln to kiln. We won't be such fools in future as to consider eagles of higher repute than ourselves. They haven't more feet or eyes than we have, and you yourself saw, this very moment, that they fly close to the ground, just like us fowls."

Tired of listening to this nonsense, the Eagle replied,

"There is something in what you say, but you're not quite right. It sometimes happens that eagles stoop even below the level of barndoor fowls, but never that such fowls soar into the clouds."

APELLES AND THE ASS COLT.

A PELLES invited to his house a young Ass whom he
happened to meet. The very bones jumped for joy
within the Donkey's frame, and it began to bore the forest
to death by its bragging, addressing the other animals in
such words as these :

"How tired I am of Apelles! I find him a regular nuisance.
Why, I never meet him but what he invites me to his house.
I suppose, my friends, that he means to paint a 'Pegasus'
from me."

"No," said Apelles, who happened to be close by ; "but
as I intend to paint a 'Judgment of Midas,' I wanted to
take your ears as a model for his; and so I shall be glad if
you will come to my house. I 've come across a good many
donkeys' ears in my time, but such splendid ones as yours
it has never been my luck to see possessed not merely by
an ass colt, but even by any full-grown ass."

[This fable is said to have been intended for the benefit
of a young author named Katenin, who, after the fabulist
had twice asked him to his house, went about saying that
Krilof was boring him with invitations.]

THE LION AND THE WOLF.

WHILE a Lion was breakfasting off a lamb, a little Dog, which was frisking around the regal table, tore away a small morsel from under the Lion's claws; and the King of Beasts passed the matter over without taking any offence. (The Dog was still young and foolish.)

A Wolf, who saw this, took it into its head that as the Lion was so patient it could not possibly be strong. And so it also laid its paw upon the lamb.

But it fared badly with the Wolf. The Wolf itself got served up at the Lion's table. The Lion tore it asunder, addressing it thus the while:

"You were wrong, my friend, to suppose, from what you saw the dog do, that I should wink at your doings also. The dog has not yet come to years of discretion, but as for you— you are no longer a mere cub."

THE RAT AND THE MOUSE.

"NEIGHBOUR! have you heard the good news?" cried a Mouse, as it came running in to a Rat. "Why, they say the cat has fallen into the clutches of the lion! So you see even we shall have a quiet breathing-time at last."

"Don't go making yourself so happy, my dear!" replied the Rat. "Indulge in no such futile hopes! If those two really do begin clawing each other, believe me, it won't be the lion which will be left alive. Than the cat there is no beast stronger."

Many a time have I seen what you may see for yourselves. When cowards fear any one, they think every one else sees in him what they do.

THE BEE AND THE FLIES.

TWO Flies determined to be off to foreign parts, and tried to entice a Bee to go there with them. They had heard from parrots high praises of distant lands. Besides, it seemed to them abominable that, on their native soil, they should everywhere be excluded from hospitality, nay, that it should even have come to this — (how is it people are not ashamed of such things? and what oddities there are in the world!)—that glass covers should have been invented to keep flies away, and prevent them from profiting by the sweets on sumptuous tables. And as to poor men's houses, why, there they found the spiders a nuisance.

"A pleasant journey to you!" replied the Bee to all this. "For my part, I am comfortable even in my own land. I have succeeded, by means of my honeycomb, in gaining the affections of all, from the villager even to the grandee. But as for you, fly whither it pleases you: you will meet with the same fate everywhere. As you are of no use, my friends, you will nowhere be either honoured or loved. There, as well as here, it will only be the spiders who will be glad to see you."

He who toils usefully for his Fatherland will not lightly desert it. But a foreign land is always pleasant to one who is destitute of useful qualities. There, as he is not a citizen, he is less despised than at home, and to no one there is his idleness a source of vexation.

THE PEASANT AND THE SNAKE.

A SNAKE once glided up to a Peasant, and said, "Neighbour, let us take to living on friendly terms. You need not be on your guard against me any longer. You can see for yourself that I have changed my skin this spring, and that I have become quite a different creature from what I was."

But the Snake did not convince the Peasant. The Peasant seized a cudgel, and cried,

"Though you 've got a new skin, yet your heart is just the same as of old."

And the neighbour's life was straightway knocked out of her.

THE EAR OF CORN.

AN Ear of Corn which shook in the wind afield —
catching sight of a flower which was fondled in comfort and luxury behind the glass of a hothouse, while it was itself exposed to troops of flies, and to heat and cold and storm—in a tone of vexation addressed its master thus :

"How comes it that you men are always so unjust that there is nothing you refuse to one who knows how to please your eye or taste, while you are utterly careless about one who is practically useful to you? Are not your chief profits derived from the corn-field? And yet, only see in what contempt it is held ! Since the day when you sowed this piece of ground, have you ever sheltered our blades under glass from bad weather, or given orders that we should be weeded or warmed, or come to water us in a drought?

"No : our growth is left entirely to chance ; whereas your flowers, which can neither fatten nor enrich you, are not, like us, left out here in the fields unheeded. They grow up within glass walls, trimly tended in a luxurious retreat. Why, if you had only taken as much pains about us instead, you would certainly have gained a hundredfold in the course of a year, and would have sent to town a whole caravan full of grain !

Do think the matter over, and build a good big hothouse to hold us."

"Friend," replied the master, "I see that you have not paid attention to my labours. Trust me, my chief care has been for you. If you only knew what pains it cost me to clear away the forest, and to have the ground manured for your benefit! Why, there was no end to my toil! But I have neither time nor inclination to talk now, nor would there be any use in my doing so. As for wind and rain, address your requests to the heavens. But your wise advice to me would, if I had followed it, have left me with neither corn nor flowers."

A WORM begged a Peasant to let it go into his garden
and spend the summer there as his guest. It promised to behave honourably, and not to touch the fruit; to
eat nothing but leaves, and those only which had already
begun to fade.

The Peasant thought, "How can I deny it a refuge?
Shall I feel cramped in my garden because there is a worm
the more in it? Let it go and live there. Besides, even if
it does eat two or three leaves, that won't be a serious loss."

He consents. The Worm crawls up a tree, finds a refuge
from bad weather under a twig, lives there, if not sumptuously, yet with all its wants supplied, and no one hears a
word about it.

Meanwhile the king of light had already gilded the fruits.
There, in that garden, where everything else was fast growing mellow, an apple, transparent, clear as amber, had fully
ripened on a twig in the sun.

Now a Boy had long been enamoured of that apple, which
he had picked out of a thousand others. But the apple was
hard to get at. To climb the apple-tree the boy did not

dare, to shake it he was not strong enough—in a word, he could not tell how to get hold of the apple.

Who helped the Boy to the theft?   The Worm.

"Listen!" it says.   "I know to a certainty that the master has ordered the apples to be gathered, so this one won't stop here long for either of us.   Still I can undertake to get it, only you must share it with me.   But you may take even ten times more than I do for your share, for a very little portion of it will take me a whole age to eat."

The Boy consented and the compact was made.   The Worm climbed up the apple-tree, set to work, and gnawed away the apple in a moment.   But what was the recompense it got?   No sooner had the apple fallen than the Boy ate it up, pips and all, and when the Worm had crawled down to get its share, the Boy crushed it under his heel.   And so there was an end of both the Worm and the apple.

I N Egypt, in the olden time, whenever people wanted to
bury any one in a very sumptuous style, it was the custom to have professional female mourners to wail behind
the coffin.

Once upon a time, at a grand funeral, a number of these
mourners, uttering loud howls, were escorting home a dead
man who had passed from this transitory life to everlasting
rest.

Then a stranger, who fancied that in them he saw the
whole family of the defunct a prey to unfeigned woe, said
to them :

"Tell me, wouldn't you be pleased if I were to bring him
to life for you?   I am a magician, and so I have the power
of doing such things.   We keep about us such exorcisms—
the corpse will come to life in a moment."

" Father," they all cried out, " pray give us poor creatures
that pleasure ! There is only one other favour we would ask
—that he may die again at the end of four or five days.
While he was alive here there was no good at all in him, and
there scarcely could be any if he were to live longer.   But

if he were to die, why, then, of course, they would have to hire us to howl for him again."

[Krilof need scarcely have gone all the way to Egypt for his "howlers." Numbers of women earn a comfortable livelihood in Russia as "crieresses," being employed not only at funerals, but also at marriages—for the bride is expected to mourn freely at having to leave her father's home, and pass from the state of "maiden liberty" to that of married subjection, and the "crieress" is invaluable as prompting her with the wailings appropriate to the occasion.]

THE COUNCIL OF THE MICE.

ONCE upon a time the Mice took it into their heads to glorify themselves, to spread abroad the fame of their deeds from the cellar to the attic, and, in spite of cats, male and female, to drive cooks and housekeepers out of their senses.

And to this end it was resolved to convene a council, in which those only should be allowed to sit whose tails were as long as the rest of their bodies.

It is acknowledged among mice that the longer a mouse's tail is, the wiser he is sure to be, and the quicker in everything. Whether this be true or not we will not inquire at present. We ourselves, for the matter of that, often judge of a man's wisdom according to the cut of his dress or his beard.

But you must know that by general consent it was decided that only long-tailed members should be admitted into the council. As for those who unfortunately had no tails, although they might have lost them in battle, yet, inasmuch as such loss is a sign of folly or carelessness, they should not be admitted into the council, in order that mice should thereby be deterred from losing their tails through their own fault.

Everything was duly arranged; it was proclaimed that the assembly would be held as soon as it was night, and finally the sitting was opened in a meal-bin.

But, as soon as the seats had been taken, there sat a rat without a tail!

A young Mouse, who saw that, turned to a grey-haired Mouse, and said,

"What right has that tailless one to sit here with us? What has become of our regulation? Call out that he may be expelled at once! You know that our people don't like the tailless. And is it likely that we could find of any use to us one who had not managed to save even his own tail? Why, he will be the ruin not only of us, but of the whole under-floor population."

But the old Mouse replied,

"Hush! I know all that; but that rat is my gossip."

[La Fontaine's fable, "Le Conseil tenu par les Rats," was translated by Khvostof, under the title adopted in the present case by Krilof, *Sozyet Muishei;* but the two fables have nothing else in common. The rat most probably represents some great man who, although disqualified for office, assumed it in an assembly of smaller people. But what his name was does not appear.]

THE LAMB.

A LAMB, which from sheer folly had donned a wolf's skin, went to the sheep-fold, there to strut about in it. The Lamb wanted merely to show itself off a little, but the dogs which saw the foolish animal thought that a wolf had broken in from the forest. In they leaped, rushed at it, knocked it off its feet, and tore it almost to pieces before it could collect its scattered wits. Luckily the shepherds recognized it and rescued it.

But it is no joke to be even for a time exposed to the teeth of dogs. After such a fright as this the poor creature could scarcely drag itself to the sheep-fold, and after it had got there its strength began to desert it, so that before long it became a perfect wreck, moaning away without cessation for the rest of its life.

But if the Lamb had been wise, it would have been afraid of becoming, even in fancy, like unto a wolf.

16—2

THE PEASANT AND THE SNAKE.

A PEASANT and a Snake became bosom friends. It is well known that snakes are clever, and this one had so crept into the Peasant's good graces, that he swore by it, and by nothing else. From that time forward, of all his former friends and relatives, not one would stir a foot towards him.

"But why," says the Peasant, reproachfully, "why have you all forsaken me? Is it that my wife hasn't known how to receive you? or have you become tired of what I have to offer you?"

"No," replied his gossip Matvei. "We'd come and see you with pleasure, neighbour; and you've never—not a word can be said against that—never once vexed or angered us in anything. But just tell me, what pleasure can one find in your house if, while one's sitting there, one can think of nothing but looking out that that friend of yours doesn't crawl up and sting some one?"

THE SPIDER AND THE BEE.

A MERCHANT brought some linen to a fair. That's a thing everybody wants to buy, so it would have been a sin in the Merchant if he had complained of his sale. There was no keeping the buyers back : the shop was at times crammed full.

Seeing how rapidly the goods went off, an envious Spider was tempted by the Merchant's gains. She took it into her head to weave goods for sale herself, and determined to open a little shop for them in a window corner, seeking thereby to undermine the Merchant's success.

She commenced her web, span the whole night long, and then set out her wares on view. From her shop she did not stir, but remained sitting there, puffed up with pride, and thinking, "So soon as the day shall dawn will all buyers be enticed to me."

Well, the day did dawn. But what then? There came a broom, and the ingenious creature and her little shop were swept clean away.

Our Spider went wild with vexation.

"There!" she cried, "what's the good of expecting a just reward? And yet I ask the whole world—Whose work is the finer, mine or that Merchant's?"

"Yours, to be sure," answered the Bee. "Who would venture to deny the fact? Every one knew that long ago. But what is the good of it if there's neither warmth nor wear in it?"

THE FEAST.

ONCE, during a year of dearth, the Lion prepared a rich feast as a means of general consolation. Couriers and heralds were sent out to invite the guests—the animals both small and great.

From all sides they crowd together on the invitation to the Lion's abode. How could such an invitation possibly be refused? A feast is a good thing even at a time which is not one of dearth.

Well, there came among others a Marmot, a Fox, and a Mole; only they came an hour after the proper time, and found that the guests were already at table. The Fox, unluckily, had had its hands full of business; the Marmot had lost a great deal of time in getting up and washing itself, and the Mole had lost its way. However, none of them were inclined to go home empty, so, spying a vacant place near the Lion, all three tried to make their way to it.

"Hark ye, brothers!" said the Panther to them; "there is plenty of room there, only it isn't intended for you. The Elephant is coming there, and he will turn you out; or, worse still, will squeeze you to death. So if you don't want to go away hungry, you will stop there on the threshold.

You will get your fill, and that's a thing to thank God for! The places in front are not for the like of you. They're kept for animals of a large size only; but those of the little ones who don't like to eat standing, had better keep their seats at home."

[This fable was not printed till 1869, when it appeared for the first time in a collection of essays, etc., about Krilof, published at St. Petersburg by the Imperial Academy of Sciences. Appended to the MS. was the following note, by a daughter of Krilof's friend and patron, Olenine.—"At the time when this fable was written by Krilof, the censors would not allow it to be printed."]

THE PEASANT AND THE DOG.

A PEASANT, who was a great economist, and the possessor of a well-to-do homestead, hired a Dog to watch his courtyard and bake his bread, and, besides all this, to hoe and water his young cabbages.

"What stuff is this he's made up?" says the reader. "There's neither rhyme nor reason in it! Let's suppose the Dog watched the courtyard. Good! But has any one ever seen dogs baking bread or watering cabbages?"

Reader! I should not have been altogether justified if I had answered in the affirmative. But the matter in question is not that, but this—that our Barbos undertook to do all these things, and demanded and got triple pay in consequence.

For Barbos this was capital. What did any one else matter?

Meanwhile the Peasant got ready for the fair, went to it, amused himself there for a time, and then came home again. At his first glance round—life became a burden to him; he tore and raged with vexation. There was no bread in the house, there were no cabbages; and, besides this, a thief had slipped into the yard and stripped the store-room bare.

On Barbos then burst a storm of abuse; but he had his excuse ready for everything. It was utterly impossible for him to bake bread on account of having to look after the cabbages. The cabbage-garden turned out a failure merely because the constant guarding of the courtyard left him without a foot to stand on. And he had not observed the thief, simply because he was at that moment preparing to bake the bread.

THE MECHANICIAN.

A CERTAIN smart young fellow bought a big house; an oldish one, it is true, but capitally constructed. The house had every merit in the way of solidity and comfort, and it would have been suited to his taste in everything had it not been for this drawback : it was rather a long way off from any water.

"Well, anyhow," he thought, " I may do what I like with my own. So I will have my house, just as it stands, moved to the river by machinery "—our friend, as you can see, had a passion for mechanics—" I shall only have to dig under its foundations, put runners under its walls, set it upon rollers, and then, by means of a windlass, comfortably handle, so to speak, the whole building, and set it down just where I like. And what's more—a thing the world has never yet seen— when my house is being moved, I will go in it to my new place of residence, riding as if in a carriage, and feasting, with friends around me, to the sound of music."

Bewitched by this folly, our Mechanician instantly set to work. He hired workmen, he dug and dug beneath his house. Neither money nor pains did he spare in the least. But he could not manage to move his house, and all that he attained to was this—that his house tumbled to pieces

THE MICE.

"OH, sister! have you heard the terrible news?" said one Mouse on board a vessel to another. "The ship must have sprung a leak! Down below there, the water has risen as high as the very tip of my snout." (But in reality she had scarcely got her paws wet.) "And no wonder! our captain is either drunk or suffering from the effects of drunkenness, and the sailors are all each one lazier than the other. In fact, there is no kind of order anywhere. I cried out immediately, and let every one know that our ship was going to the bottom. What was the use? No one lent me an ear, just as if I had been spreading false news. But the fact is plain enough: one has only to look into the hold to see that the ship has not another hour to live. Surely, sister, it is not good that we should perish with the rest? Come, let us fling ourselves at once from the ship! Perchance the land is not far off."

With that our strange friends sprang into the sea, and —were drowned. But the ship, steered by a skilful hand, reached the harbour safe and sound.

Now will come questions: "But how about the captain, and the sailors, and the leak?"

The leak was a little one, and besides, it was stopped immediately. But the rest—was mere calumny.

[It is not clear to what this fable, which was first printed in 1833, has special reference, but Trutofsky's illustration of it will serve to give an idea of its general meaning. Two ladies of the landed proprietor class are talking about the emancipation of the serfs. One of them has in her hand a copy of the famous decree of February 19, 1861, by which serfdom was abolished in Russia, and is evidently whispering fearful forebodings into the ear of the other, who holds up her hands in horror. From a corner of the room a barefooted peasant girl quietly watches the two terrified ladies. The slaveholding Mice evidently think that the ship of the State is sinking fast.]

THE FALCON AND THE CATERPILLAR.

A CATERPILLAR was swinging to and fro on a twig to which it had attached itself on the top of a tree. A Falcon floating in the air above it thus mocked and flouted it from on high :

"What toils, poor thing, must thou not have endured! And what profits it that thou hast climbed so high? What freedom hast thou, and what kind of independence? Thou must always bend with the twig whichever way the wind orders."

"It is easy for thee to scoff," answers the Caterpillar. "Thou flyest high because thou art stoutly built and strong in the wings. But it is not such merits as those that Fate has given me. Here on this height I hold my own simply because I am, fortunately, tenacious."

A SNAKE begged Jupiter to bestow upon her the voice of a nightingale.

"As I am," she says, "my life is hateful to me. Where-ever I show myself, all who are weaker than I am are fright-ened at the sight of me. And as to those who are stronger, God grant that I may escape from them alive! No, such a life as this I can no longer endure. But if I could sing in the forest like a nightingale, then, exciting admiration, I should obtain love and, perhaps, respect, and would become the life of festive meetings."

Jupiter granted the Snake's request. Not even a trace of her hideous hissing was retained by her. The Snake glided up a tree, chose a resting-place upon it, and began to sing as beautifully as any nightingale.

The birds flocked together from all sides, and would have perched close by her; but as soon as they caught sight of the songstress, away they all flew from the tree in a body. Whom could such a reception please?

"Is it possible you can find my voice disagreeable?" asks the Snake with vexation.

"No," replies a Starling: "it is sonorous, wonderful. In

fact, you sing as well as the nightingale.   But, to tell the truth, our hearts shuddered within us when we saw your sting.   To us it is a terrible thing to be in your company. And so I will say this to you, but not with any intention of annoying you.   We shall be delighted to hear your songs, only sing them at a little distance from us."   ,

THE HARE AT THE CHASE.

HAVING united in full force, the beasts captured a
bear. They strangled it in the open, and then
began to settle among themselves what part each of them
should get as his share.

But at this point the Hare, forsooth, clutches the bear's
ear.

"Hallo! you squinter there!" they shout at him. "Where
on earth have you come from? No one has seen you during
the chase."

"Really now, brothers!" answered the Hare. "And who
was it, if you please, who drove him out of the wood? Didn't

I frighten him entirely, and drive him, this dear friend of ours, right afield to you?"

Such bragging was somewhat too palpable, it is true, but it had such an amusing air about it, that, the Hare was presented with a morsel of the bear's ear.

[It has often been said that Krilof alluded in this fable to the fact of Austria having joined the Allied Powers after they had overthrown Napoleon, and then demanded her share of the spoil.

But this can scarcely be, as the fable appeared in the summer of 1813, during the heat of the war for the independence of Germany. It is very probable that subsequently, at the time of the Congress of Vienna, the fable was quoted in reference to the acquisitive tendencies displayed by Austria, and this may have given rise to the idea that Krilof had that Power in view when he wrote it.]

THE PEASANT AND THE FOX.

SAID a Fox to a Peasant, one day:
"Tell me, my dear gossip, what has the horse done to deserve such friendship at your hands, that, as I see, he is always by your side? You keep him in plenty and well cared for. When journeying, you go along with him, and with him you constantly go afield. And yet, of all animals, he surely is all but the stupidest!"

"Ah, gossip!" replied the Peasant, "this isn't a question of wisdom: all that's mere stuff. That isn't at all what I go in for. What I want is that he should carry me and obey the whip."

THE SHEPHERD.

THE shepherd Savva had charge of a Seigneur's flocks. Suddenly the sheep began to disappear.

Our fine fellow is plunged in grief and woe. Everywhere he goes weeping and spreading abroad the news that a terrible wolf has appeared—that it has taken to dragging the sheep from the fold and pitilessly tearing them to pieces.

"And there's nothing wonderful in that," say the people. "What pity have wolves for sheep?"

So they take to watching for the wolf.

But how comes it that our dear Savva's oven can now boast of cabbage soup with mutton in it, or say a sheep's side and *kasha* *? (He had been turned out of a scullion's place, and sent into the fields as a shepherd, by way of punishment for his faults: so he kept a kitchen more like one of ours than a peasant's.)

A great search is made for the wolf: it is cursed on all sides, and the whole forest is rummaged for it. But not a trace of it can be found.

Friends, your trouble is of no use. About the wolf it's all mere talk. The real devourer of the sheep is—Savva.

---

* A favourite dish made of buckwheat.

THE CARP.

A NUMBER of carp dwelt in the clear spring-water of a lake in a Seigneur's garden. In shoals they used to sport near the banks, and all their days, it seemed, went by like days of gold.

But suddenly the Seigneur orders a number of pike to be put in the pond with them.

"Excuse me!" says a friend of his, who heard of that, "excuse me, but what can you be intending to do? What good thing can ever come of a pike? Not a fin will be left of the carp to a certainty. Can it be that you don't know how voracious pike are?"

"Don't waste your words," smilingly answers the Seigneur. "I'm well aware of all that. But I should like to know what makes you think that I am fond of carp?"

THE HIGHWAYMAN AND THE WAGGONER.

ONE day, towards nightfall, a Highwayman was lying in wait for booty in a thicket, at a little distance from a road. And as a hungry bear looks out from its den, so did he gaze gloomily into the distance.

Presently he sees a lumbering waggon come rolling on like a wave.

"Ah!" whispers our Highwayman. "Laden, no doubt, with goods for the fair: nothing but cloth, and damask, and brocade, to a certainty. Don't stand gaping at it: there you'll get wherewithal to live. Ah! this day will not be lost for me!"

Meanwhile the waggon arrives. "Stop!" cries the robber, and flings himself upon the driver, cudgel in hand. But, unluckily for him, it was no mere lubberly lad he had to do with. The Waggoner was a strapping youth, who confronted the malefactor with a big stick, and defended his goods like a mountain.

Our hero was obliged to fight hard for his prey. The battle was long and fierce. The robber lost a dozen teeth, and had an arm smashed and an eye knocked out. But, in spite of all this, he remained the victor.

The malefactor killed the Waggoner — killed him, and rushed upon the spoil. What did he get? A whole waggon-load of bladders!

THE RICH MAN AND THE POET.

A POET lodged an action against an exceedingly rich man, and entreated Jupiter to take his side. Both parties were ordered to appear in court. They came: the one lean and hungry, barely clothed, barely shod : the other all over gold and all puffed up by conceit.

"Take pity on me," cries the Poet, "O Ruler of Olympus! Cloud-compeller, hurler of thunderbolts! in what have I sinned before thee, that from my youth upwards I have endured the cruel persecutions of Fortune? No spoon is mine to feed from, no corner to lie in, and all my possessions exist in fancy alone. Meanwhile my rival, who has neither mind nor merit, has been living in palaces surrounded by a herd of worshippers, just as if he were an idol of thine, and swimming in the fat of luxurious delicacy!"

"But is it nothing," replied Jupiter, "that the sounds of thy lyre will resound to a distant age, while he will not be remembered by his grandsons, not to speak of his great-grandsons? Didst not thou thyself choose glory as thy share? To him I gave the good things of this world during his lifetime. But, believe me, if he had understood things better, and if his mind could possibly have appreciated his insignificance compared with thee, he would have grumbled at his lot more than thou art grumbling at thine."

THE SNAKE AND THE LAMB.

A SNAKE lay beneath a log, and raged against the whole world. It had no other feeling in it than that of rage. Of such a kind had Nature created it. Hard by there bounded and frolicked a Lamb: it never even so much as thought about the Snake.

But see! the Snake comes gliding up and strikes its fangs into the Lamb. The sky grows dark before the poor thing's eyes, and the poison turns all its blood into fire.

"What harm have I done thee?" it says to the Snake.

"Who knows?" hisses out the Snake. "It may be that thou hast stolen hither to crush me. It is by way of pre-caution that I punish thee."

"Ah, no!" replies the Lamb—and then its life deserts it.

One whose heart is so framed that it knows neither friend-ship nor love, and nourishes only hatred towards all men, such a one considers every man his enemy.

THE NIGHTINGALES.

A CERTAIN birdcatcher one spring had caught a number of Nightingales in the copses. The songsters were put in cages, and they began to sing, although they would much rather have been wandering at will through the woods. When one sits in prison, has one a mind for song? But there was nothing to be done; so they sang, some from sorrow, and others to pass the time.

One poor wretch among the Nightingales endured more suffering than any of the others. He had been taken from his mate: to him confinement was most grievous. Through his tears he looked out afield from his cage; day and night did he sorrow.

At last he thinks "Grief cures no evil. Only fools weep on account of misfortunes; the wise seek for the means of working out relief from their woes. I, too, methinks, will be able to fling this weight of calamity off my neck. Surely we cannot have been caught for eating. Our master, I can see, likes to hear singing. So if I do him a service by my voice, it may be that it will bring me my reward, and he will put an end to my captivity."

So thought our minstrel, and began to sing. With song he glorified the evening glow, and with song he greeted the

18

rising of the sun.   But what finally came to pass?   He thereby only aggravated his hard fate.   For the birds who sang badly their master has long ago opened wide both cage and window, letting them all go free.   But as to our poor Nightingale, the more sweetly, the more tenderly it sings, the more strictly is it looked after.

[Trutofsky's illustration of this fable represents the interior of a Government office.   It is closing-time, and the ordinary clerks are getting ready to leave.   The model clerk still sits at his table with a gloomy expression on his face.   His chief is handing him a thick bundle of documents.   The good singer is being kept in his cage.]

THE END.

INDEX TO THE FABLES.

—o—

Cassell & Company, Limited, Belle Sauvage Works, London, E.C.

www.ingramcontent.com/pod-product-compliance
Lightning Source LLC
Chambersburg PA
CBHW031400270326
41929CB00010BA/1263